D1562464

JOURNAL FOR THE STUDY OF THE OLD TESTAMENT
SUPPLEMENT SERIES

94

Editors
David J A Clines
Philip R Davies

JSOT Press
Sheffield

What Does Eve Do to Help?

and Other Readerly Questions to the Old Testament

David J. A. Clines

Journal for the Study of the Old Testament
Supplement Series 94

Copyright © 1990 Sheffield Academic Press

Published by JSOT Press
JSOT Press is an imprint of
Sheffield Academic Press Ltd
The University of Sheffield
343 Fulwood Road
Sheffield S10 3BP
England

Printed in Great Britain
by Billing & Sons Ltd
Worcester

British Library Cataloguing in Publication Data

Clines, David J.A.
    What does Eve do to help?
    1. Bible. O.T. —Critical studies
    I. Title   II. Series
    221.6

    ISSN 0309-0787
    ISBN 1-85075-248-6

CONTENTS

For

Cheryl
David
David
Elizabeth
George
Jim
Tamara
Walter

and

my other
conversation-partners
in the
Society of Biblical Literature

High thanks I owe you, excellent friends,
who carry out the world for me to new and noble heights,
and enlarge the meaning of all my thoughts.

—Emerson

ABBREVIATIONS

AB	Anchor Bible
BHK	*Biblia Hebraica*, ed. R. Kittel (3rd edn; Stuttgart: Württemburgische Bibelanstalt, 1937)
BHS	*Biblia Hebraica Stuttgartensia*, ed. K. Elliger and W. Rudolph (Stuttgart: Deutsche Bibelstiftung, 1966-67)
BZAW	Beiheft zur *Zeitschrift für die alttestamentliche Wissenschaft*
CambB	Cambridge Bible
CBQ	*Catholic Biblical Quarterly*
CentB	Century Bible
DSB	The Daily Study Bible
ExpB	The Expositor's Bible
FOTL	The Forms of the Old Testament Literature
GNB	Good News Bible
HAT	Handbuch zum Alten Testament
HTR	*Harvard Theological Review*
ICC	International Critical Commentary
Interp	*Interpretation*
ITC	International Theological Commentary
JAAR	*Journal of the American Academy of Religion*
JAOS	*Journal of the American Oriental Society*
JSOT	*Journal for the Study of the Old Testament*
JSOTSup	*Journal for the Study of the Old Testament, Supplement Series*
NCB	New Century Bible
NICOT	New International Commentary on the Old Testament
OTL	Old Testament Library
SBL	Society of Biblical Literature
SBLMS	Society of Biblical Literature Monograph Series
TBC	Torch Bible Commentary
TOTC	Tyndale Old Testament Commentaries
USQR	*Union Seminary Quarterly Review*
WBC	Word Biblical Commentary
WC	Westminster Commentaries
ZAW	*Zeitschrift für die alttestamentliche Wissenschaft*

INTRODUCTION

Rather than speaking abstractly of poetry,
which is a form of ennui or loafing ...

Jorge Luis Borges[1]

I

Readerly questions are raised when readers are explicitly and programmatically brought into the process of interpreting texts. Traditionally, the reader and readerly interests and identities have been screened out when we have set about interpreting texts, and we have set our sights on attaining an interpretation that should be as 'objective' as possible. We have long recognized that all interpretations are interfered with to a greater or lesser degree by the person of the interpreter, but in the past we have endeavoured to minimize that interference.

Things are rather different now. Not only is the quest for an objective interpretation seen as a chimaera, but the rewards of unabashed 'readerly' interpretations that foreground the process of reading and the context of the reader have now been shown to be well worth seeking. As the culture of those who read and interpret the Bible becomes more pluralist, it becomes less and less plausible to lay claim to determinate interpretations and more valuable to read the Bible afresh from the perspectives of different readers. And as we become increasingly alert to readers' contribution to the creation of meaning, it is more than ever essential to raise readerly questions.

What has happened in Biblical studies, as likewise in many branches of literary studies in the last three decades, can be represented, rather simply, as a shift in focus that has moved

---

1 Jorge Luis Borges, *Seven Nights* (tr. Eliot Weinberger; London: Faber and Faber, 1986), p. 82.

from *author* to *text* to *reader*.

The traditional questions, which were still in Old Testament studies at least, the only scholarly questions that were being asked in the 1960s, were questions of philology and history, questions which put the author in the centre of the picture. They asked, What did he (it was always he) mean, when did he live, what did he know, what sources did he use, what was his intention? The meaning of the text was always and exclusively what it meant, what it meant to the 'original author'. These were the questions I as a student was trained to ask, and these are the questions which the introductions and commentaries and theologies of that time all took for granted, Eissfeldt, Eichrodt, and von Rad.

Some, it is true, like Krister Stendahl in a famous article, distinguished between what the text meant and what it means, between exegesis and application.[1] But what it means was always the poor relation, always subject to the scornful stern finger pointing to the door by the haughty lord of the manor, Sir What It Meant. There were many, and they seemed to be in the positions of power, who maintained that 'what it means' is not actually a scholarly question; it could be left to second-rate intellects to consider the application of pure, basic, fundamental research on 'what it meant'.

There were two things wrong with this author-centred approach. First, it could always be protested that the historical-critical method systematically regarded the biblical text as a window through which to scrutinize something other than the text, namely historical actuality. There was nothing wicked about this, unless perhaps it was being claimed that this was all there was to studying the Bible. But certainly it was sad, because the text was being crowded out, in favour of another subject of study, historical actuality. Secondly, a wave of uncertainty, from the late 1960s onward, was sweeping the scholarly world about all sorts of historical-critical conclusions (the sources of the Pentateuch, the Israelite amphictyony, the Solomonic Enlightenment, and so on), and one needed strong

1 Krister Stendahl, 'Biblical Theology', in *The Interpreter's Dictionary of the Bible*, ed. George A. Buttrick (Nashville: Abingdon, 1962), vol. 1, pp. 418-32 (esp. 430-31).

nerves to go on insisting there was no problem.

The obvious move was to shift the focus from the author to the text. Now the subject of study tended to become, not what the author meant, but what the text means. After all, the text, like the poor, was always with us. We could get on with the text and its meaning, while leaving historical questions for antiquarians. This was a very 1970s thing to do in Biblical studies. It was immensely rewarding, and there still remain vast areas of the biblical text to be explored by this approach. It involves the study of themes, images, character, plot, style, metaphor, point of view, narrators, readers implied and real, and so on.

Among the principal concerns of a text-oriented approach were these: 1. It aimed to establish the meaning of a text by reading the text rather than by asking what the author intended. 2. It emphasized the work as a whole, which involved the elucidation of the whole in relation to its parts and of the parts in relation to the whole. 3. It resisted a romantic view of texts as essentially the 'expression' of an author, or as affording an insight into the psychology of a great thinker or artist. It recognizes that texts are entities existing in the world, and deserving of study in their own right, regardless of the circumstances of their composition.

There were faults in this approach too. Among them may be noted: 1. A certain lack of 'engagement with real life'. If we concentrate upon the text, it is all too easy for the text to be severed from the past, to be idealized, to be regarded as a free-floating object. And, what is more serious, under cover of this professed preoccupation with the text itself, the critic was still able to slip in any number of his or her own prejudices, especially concerning which texts were worth studying. In English literature, New Criticism, from which the text-oriented approach in Biblical studies drew much of its inspiration, often hid right-wing values, while in Biblical studies, canonical criticism, for example, which might be seen as a kind of New Criticism, brought with it implicit messages about the authority of the Church. 2. Even more serious, focus on the text left out the reader. In the making of meaning, readers have a vital part. For we cannot say, This text is meaningful, but it means nothing to me or you or anyone. No doubt, readers do not

make up meanings, or, if we do, we say they are bad readers.
But, on the other hand, texts themselves do not have meanings
which readers then proceed to discover. In some way or other,
the creation of meaning arises at the intersection between text
and reader.

So, in the 1980s, the focus in literary studies has come to be
on the reader. All readers of texts, including Biblical texts,
bring their own interests, prejudices and presuppositions with
them. While they would be wrong to insist that the Bible
should say what they want it to say, they would be equally
wrong to think that it does not matter, in reading the Bible,
what they themselves already believe. For the combination of
the reader's own interests, values and commitments is what
makes him or her a person with identity and integrity; in no
activity of life, and certainly not in reading the Bible, can one
hide or abandon one's values without doing violence to one's
own integrity. If one is, for example, a feminist pacifist vegetarian—which are quite serious things to be, even if they happen to be modish (so is believing in God and being against slav-
ery, but we don't snigger)—, it will be important to oneself to
ask what the text has to say, or fails to say, about these issues;
one will recognize that the text may have little concern with
such matters, but if they are a serious concern to the reader
they may be legitimately put on the agenda for interpretation,
that is, the mutual activity that goes on between text and
reader. And what usually happens, when we bring our questions to the text instead of insisting always that the text set the
agenda, is that the text becomes illuminated in unpredictable
ways.

II

What particular characteristics, then, of the manner of reading by this reader will be presented in this volume? I need to
say that although I am interested in literary theory and the
theory of reading, I do not usually proceed from a theoretical
position when I set about the business of reading. To be sure, I
learn from others what kind of things I might be looking for
when I am reading, and with the help of other writers
sharpen my perception of my own positions and commit-

ments; but when I read I am on my own. Certainly, I play off other people's readings, and find other readings mostly helpful when I can distinguish mine from them; I especially like insensitive and wooden commentators, because they quite often stumble conspicuously over facets of a text that are really there but which they do not know how to deal with; more sophisticated commentators know how to slide over things they find difficult. All the same, I do not like to stay on my own for too long, but, like most of us, crave the approval of some reputable scholarly circle. So I like to check out from time to time what I have been doing against what more philosophically and systematically inclined theorists have been saying about the business of interpretation. And it is especially those who have paid attention to readers and reading whom I have found congenial; I must therefore, I tell myself, have been adopting a readerly orientation.

The first thing that a readerly orientation will concern itself with is the *process of reading*. Traditionally, reading has been a quite transparent activity, like breathing, which we either do not think about or, if we do, believe we understand it quite well. A readerly concern, by contrast, problematizes reading— which is to say, wonders what it is that is going on, and how whatever it is actually works.

So one of my interests in this volume is what happens to us as readers when we try to match in our reading the linear shape of a book. Books are usually designed by authors, publishers and social conventions to be read from beginning to end, and that is how most readers approach them, especially if they are narrative works and not, say, encyclopaedias. A readerly interest therefore takes seriously the fact that a typical reader will read any particular book in a linear fashion, and will not, for example, know on page 1 how the story will have developed by page 200. The reader may indeed return to the book, and read it again from cover to cover in the knowledge of how it will turn out in the end, or may, after a first reading, dip into the book at odd places, secure in a knowledge of the overall plot and structure of the book and confident of how the page before the eyes fits in to the total pattern. But it is a more common feature of our readerly experience to be first-time readers, who know nothing of what is in the book except what

we have read so far. Even second-time reading itself can in
fact often be quite like first-time reading, for we may have
forgotten how the book is going to develop, or we may have
failed to notice significant details on our first reading, or we
may be deliberately suppressing our knowledge of what lies
ahead of us for the pleasure of re-living our first experience of
excitement, involvement or absorption in the book. So first-
time reading is not a fixed moment in our experience of a book;
it can be a kind of paradisal encounter that we attempt, or
manage accidentally, to recreate.

There is a little more to the philosophy of first-time reading
than a mere description of what actually happens to readers,
however. Readers who pretend to be first-time readers sometimes justify that pretence by appealing to a certain sense of
fitness they feel about adapting themselves to the linear nature
of the book, which necessarily proceeds by increments and not
with hindsight. First-time reading, they suspect, is truly
respectful of the sequentiality of the book; and at the same time
they often feel that they will be more receptive to the promises
the book holds out before them, if they will screen off much of
the knowledge they already have, including knowledge of the
book as a whole, and content themselves with what they have
learnt from the book *so far*. If they feel that, they are responding to the book's invitation to enter its world.

Among the papers in this collection, 'What Happens in
Genesis' takes this approach most programmatically, asking
what we are led, on a first-time reading of the book, to expect
will happen, and asking thereafter whether our expectations
have been met or have been disappointed by the time we reach
the end of the book. Perhaps the way the story develops will
lead us to re-adjust or re-evaluate the expectations we originally formed, or perhaps it will confirm us in our original
understanding; but either way, in this particular case at least,
the outcome appears to justify the method, because it brings to
the surface a range of issues that have not usually been
addressed in the scholarly literature.

In 'The Ancestor in Danger' the accent is equally on 'the
story so far', but the angle of approach is different. Rather
than survey the whole of the literary work from beginning to
end, I begin with three isolated segments of it, the tales of the

ancestral couple in danger in foreign lands. Here my aim is to show that we can best understand these tales, not by considering them first in connection with one another (as their similarity has persuaded most scholars to do), but by locating each at its distinctive point in the developing plot of Genesis, and establishing the function of each by tracking the threads that link it to what has already been told in the narrative. And in 'What Does Eve Do to Help?' I fasten again upon the data of the preceding narrative as the essential and primary clue to the meaning of a disputed text.

A second concern of a readerly orientation is a reflex of the first, namely a heightened interest in the process of *writing*. For in order to appreciate well how readers read, it is important to understand how writers write, and what writerly guiles they can employ to make readers read in one way rather than another. This is not a particularly novel interest, of course, for Old Testament scholars of every stripe have long been interested in the mechanics of composition of the texts they study. Nevertheless, there is evidently a lot more attention being paid these days to the 'poetics' or art of writing, and very much more elaborated theoretical analyses of what actually goes on in the writing process. It is now part of the critical vocabulary of the Old Testament scholar, though it was not even as recently as two decades ago, to distinguish between author and narrator, narratee and implied reader, ideal reader and actual reader, and so on. And there is no question in my mind but that such conceptualizations as are represented by this terminology give us a much closer control over the processes of both writing and reading.

Such interests come to the fore especially in the essay on Nehemiah and the 'Perils of Autobiography'. In it I try to discover what difference it makes to our reading of the 'Nehemiah Memoir' that is embedded in our Book of Nehemiah if we distinguish systematically between Nehemiah the author and Nehemiah the narrator. The results of such a readerly investigation turn out to be not only literary in character—which is no more than one would expect—but, perhaps surprisingly, to have useful historical implications. I argue that in the case of the Nehemiah Memoir the narrator claims the kind of knowledge that we usually grant to an

omniscient narrator, but that, since the narrator of the
autobiography is nothing but the flesh and blood author, he has
no right to make such claims. The history of scholarship
evidences an uncritical confusion between author and narrator, with consequent misjudgments about the probable course
of historical actuality. Here is one case, then, where readerly
concerns impinge constructively upon quite different scholarly interests.

The third concern of a readerly orientation is the *social
location* of the reader. Up to this point I have been discussing
the activity of reading as a essentially private and personal
undertaking, and have been wondering about what goes on in
the lone reader's head during the process, and how that reading activity is determined by the writerly activity that preceded it. But there is of course another dimension to the reading process, which consists of the constraints and opportunities
afforded individual readers by the social context in which they
find themselves. These social contexts may be very much
broader than the activity of reading itself, of course. For
example, a feminist location commits a person to a wide range
of activities that have nothing to do with reading; and one
could easily be a feminist and take little interest in reading. In
this context, however, I am naturally concerned only with the
implications of such social locations for the way readers read.
And there are other locations which may have little existence
outside the activity of reading, such as that of the collective of
scholarly interpreters of the text, who may or may not have
any institutional or personal connections with one another but
may communicate solely through writing and on the subject
of reading and how they read. So what I mean by 'social location' is very like what people mean by 'interpretative community', except that I am giving an explicit recognition to the
fact that many such communities exist primarily for purposes
other than interpreting, and it would be wrong to think of
them as being defined by their interest in interpreting.

One such location or interpretative community in which I
am interested, and within which the present papers were
written, is the scholarly community of Old Testament specialists. These people differ from other readers of the Old Testament in that they do not on principle read just for themselves

and their own understanding, enlightenment, or benefit, but are committed to dialogue with other readers of the same community with a view to persuading others, or being persuaded by them, to read in one way rather than another. When they are reading novels or poetry they probably do not have any such commitment, and then they behave like most readers of most writing. Perhaps sometimes they may be reading the Old Testament without regard for the community of Old Testament specialists; they may be reading for their own personal edification or with some intention directed toward some religious community, and perhaps they will not always know exactly when they are reading as scholars and when they are not; for they will, in many cases, unavoidably remain scholars even when they are not reading as scholars. Nevertheless, I would maintain that there is such a thing as scholarly reading, and that those who engage in it thereby constitute an interpretative community.

Focusing upon the scholarly community of interpreters is a particular interest in the chapter on the Nehemiah Memoir. There I try to show how what counts as an acceptable reading of the Nehemiah material is very largely conditioned by the habits and preferences of previous commentators and biblical scholars. That is not very surprising, and it is a common feature of scholarly writing that it observes lines of relationship and dependence between literary works, both those of modern interpreters as well as the primary texts themselves. What is perhaps a little different about my treatment of the Nehemiah text is that I approach the habits of the interpretative community with a question about the responsibility of the *author* for the readings sanctioned by the community of his interpreters. That question is, What has the author Nehemiah done in his writing to ensure that modern readers, even critical scholarly readers, will accept, in large measure, his presentation of events and his inevitably one-sided perspective on their significance? So the issue becomes one of the complicity of the readers with the author, an often unspoken agreement, for example, to give him the benefit of the doubt. Being able to name these readers as a distinct 'community' relativizes the value of their interpretations, and gives permission to fresh interpretations to breathe, while being alerted to the tricks of

the authorial trade enables us to create some readerly de-
fences against writerly wiles.

The scholarly community is of course not one undifferentiated whole. Within it are many interest groups. One of those,
deconstructionism, provides a context for the chapter on Job,
where the question is put whether the book of Job does not
open itself to a deconstruction. In two major areas I believe I
have shown that it does, undermining in some manner views
that it also affirms. Where I hope in this essay to have served
the interest of the wider scholarly community, and not just of
deconstructionists, is in having asked the question, What happens after a text has been deconstructed?, and to have
answered that in a way that respects the actual experience of
readers.

An interpretative community of a different kind whose
interests are evident in these essays is Christianity. While it is
possible on certain issues in Old Testament studies, such as
philology or historical reconstruction, to avoid any impact of
the reader's religious commitment or lack of it upon what we
write, in strictly interpretational matters, especially large-
scale ones, it seems to be impossible. In 'The Old Testament
Histories' I discuss the most striking of the constraints the
reader's religious affiliation imposes upon interpretation,
namely, the determination of the very identity and contents of
the subject matter of our study. Is it the 'Old Testament' that
we are concerned with, or the 'Tanakh'? If it is the 'Old Testament', is it the Catholic or the Protestant Old Testament? If
it is the Hebrew Bible, why is it not the Greek Bible? If it is the
'Bible', which community's Bible is it? There is no neutral or
religiously uncommitted term for the primary texts of our
discipline; every time I open my mouth about the subject of my
professional competence I proclaim willy-nilly my religious
identity. Even if I profess no religious commitment whatsoever I am compelled to adopt someone else's even in order to
name my subject.

What is to be done about this state of affairs? We could
deplore it, and determine to paper over the cracks between the
religious communities by settling on a name that disguised the
realities. But our interpretational praxis itself, such as
whether we include the New Testament in our frame of ref-

erence when we are reading the 'Old', or the degree to which
we cite parallels from the 'Apocryphal' books, will immediately give the game away. It is very much more in keeping
with what we are recognizing these days about the social locations of interpreters that we should acknowledge the religious
contexts in which we find ourselves by choice or accident, and
not apologize for them but capitalize on them. How far I set out
deliberately to serve the interests of the interpretative community in which I am located is up to me, and I may decide
differently at different times; and in any case what is actually
in the interests of my Christian interpretative community is
itself a highly problematic matter, and hardly to be settled on
the criterion of what is familiar or comfortable to that community. But I certainly resist the idea that one's context is
essentially some kind of constraint that inevitably limits one's
interpretative vision and the interpretative possibilities open to
oneself as a reader. There are indeed constraints, but a imagination that is sympathetic to the particularities of other people's contexts can to a large extent compensate for them.
Much rather I would regard the context of an interpretative
community as offering a series of interpretative opportunities.
Just as the reading of the Old Testament in the early Christian
church gave rise to the varied and creative Christological
interpretations of it by the Church Fathers, so also the reading
of the Old Testament in feminist and Marxist interpretative
communities, to name no others, creates fresh opportunities
for meaning in our own time.

In accord with this readerly recognition of the constraints
and challenges of a religiously determined location, I have
addressed myself in the chapter on 'The Old Testament
Histories' to the question of what it can mean for Christians to
have within their scriptures two so fundamentally different
memories of the past as are enshrined within the Primary
and the Secondary Histories. I do not have much of an answer
to the question, but I think that the posing of it could in itself be
creative for a Christian notion of what a 'scripture' can be, as
well as for the less religiously-oriented question of how we
readers, as individuals or as members of a community, can
evaluate our own personal past. In the chapter on 'What Does
Eve Do to Help?' I have likewise raised the question of how a

feminist reading of the early chapters of Genesis can be accommodated within a Christian view of the Bible; again the issue of the nature of the Bible in the Christian church, and especially the matter of 'authority', comes to the fore. These Christian opportunities are not the primary purpose of these essays; but they may serve as examples of how a legitimate focus on the reader (this reader, in this case) may affect the interpretative process.

Yet another interpretative community whose interests are represented to some extent in this volume is that of feminism. The first of the essays addresses feminist readers of the Old Testament in an attempt to ground feminist interpretation more securely. It argues that the programme of 'redeeming the text' for feminism by exposing its latent egalitarian tendencies is not really successful in the case of Genesis 1–3 (though it may well be elsewhere), and that a mature feminist criticism will find these chapters to be irredeemably androcentric. In the essay on 'The Ancestor in Danger' there is likewise a feminist orientation to a set of tales which have perhaps been too readily viewed from a male perspective. Here again, the identification of an interpretative community with its own recognizable interests proves to offer a fruitful line of approach to the text.

Many other interpretative communities, at different moments in history from our own, have of course been interested in our texts. So it is a matter of interest to readerly critics to discover and understand how such communities, including those now defunct, have read. Accordingly, in the essay on 'The Old Testament Histories' there are some reflections on how the historiographical books of the Old Testament have been read in the past by the Jewish and Christian religious communities, and in the chapter on 'What Does Eve Do to Help?' I have found myself more in accord with the interpretation of Genesis by some of the fathers of the Christian church than with those of some feminist critics of our own day, with whom I am on most other matters much more in sympathy. Such an interest in other interpretative communities beside the ones to which one belongs oneself is usually subsumed under the heading of 'reception history' or 'the history of interpretation'. I for my part, however, would prefer to label

this subject 'comparative interpretation'. For although interpreters and their communities can indeed be distinguished
from one another in a historical dimension and have always
been affected by their historical circumstances, the interesting
questions that can be asked of their interpretations from a
readerly point of view are not historical questions at all, like
causes, effects and influences, but strictly interpretational
ones. Arranging the material of an intellectual discourse on
simple historical lines is often the laziest way of organizing it;
and identifying who influenced whom to say what when is not
a very deep form of enquiry. The harder and more valuable
question, at least from the reader's point of view, is whether
there is any mileage left in the interpretations of others, and
whether our own reading can be facilitated or improved by
recourse to those of others, even others from alien historical
circumstances. I foresee the emergence of a new lease of life
for so-called 'pre-critical' interpretations when they are
removed from the dominating historical paradigm, with its
implicit allegiance to the myth of progress that puts us at the
apex and our predecessors at the foot of the pyramid of
learning.

Those readers of these essays who have some acquaintance
with modern literary theory will have little difficulty in typify-
ing this book as an example of 'reader-response criticism'. I
have avoided referring to this critical approach up to this point
because I wanted to say in my own words what it is I think I
have been doing in these essays without necessarily subscrib-
ing to anyone else's theoretical programme. But I may as well
confess now that, in their various ways, the present collection
of essays belongs to that rather amorphous body of writing
that goes under the name of reader-response criticism.

Among the practitioners of reader-response I find Stanley
Fish one of the most congenial. He defined his programme as
'the rigorous and disinterested asking of the question, what
does this word, phrase, sentence, paragraph, chapter, novel,
play, poem, *do*?; and the execution involves *an analysis of the
developing response of the reader in relation to the words as
they succeed one another in time*'.[1] Literature is a kinetic art,

1 Stanley E. Fish, 'Literature in the Reader: Affective Stylistics', *New*

he says, even though the physical reality of books sitting on shelves may suggest otherwise; our experience of reading books is in fact one of movement, from beginning to end. Fish is also the originator of the notion of the 'interpretive community'.[1] And these two ideas are obviously very important to my own approach.

For the sake of the reader who wishes to pursue further the critical theory, I may say that among surveys of the progress and characteristics of reader-response criticism, I know of nothing more perceptive and lucid than that of Jane P. Tompkins in the introduction to her anthology.[2] As for the other works that I have used for orientation, stimulus, and reflection, I limit myself here to listing them in a note.[3]

Literary History 2 (Autumn, 1970), pp. 123-62 (= his *Self-Consuming Artifacts* [Berkeley: University of California Press, 1972], pp. 383-427).

1 Stanley E. Fish, 'Interpreting the *Variorum*', *Critical Inquiry* 2 (1976), pp. 465-85; reprinted in his *Is There a Text in this Class? The Authority of Interpretive Communities* (Cambridge, MA: Harvard University Press, 1980), pp. 147-73, and in Tompkins, *Reader-Response Criticism*, pp. 164-84 (182-84).

2 *Reader-Response Criticism. From Formalism to Post-Structuralism* (Baltimore: Johns Hopkins University Press, 1980).

3 Elizabeth Freund, *The Return of the Reader. Reader-response Criticism* (London: Methuen, 1987); Susan R. Suleiman and Inge Crosman, *The Reader in the Text. Essays on Audience and Interpretation* (Princeton: Princeton University Press, 1980); William Ray, *Literary Meaning. From Phenomenology to Deconstruction* (Oxford: Basil Blackwell, 1984); Edgar V. McKnight, *Post-Modern Use of the Bible. The Emergence of Reader-Oriented Criticism* (Nashville: Abingdon, 1988).

Among more wide-ranging works, I have used: David Lodge (ed.), *Modern Criticism and Theory. A Reader* (London: Longman, 1988); Edgar V. McKnight, *The Bible and the Reader. An Introduction to Literary Criticism* (Philadelphia: Fortress, 1985); Rick Rylance (ed.), *Debating Texts. A Reader in Twentieth-Century Literary Theory and Method* (Milton Keynes: Open University Press, 1987); Terry Eagleton, *Literary Theory. An Introduction* (Oxford: Basil Blackwell, 1983); D.W. Fokkema and Elrud Kunne-Ibsch, *Theories of Literature in the Twentieth Century. Structuralism, Marxism, Aesthetics of Reception, Semiotics* (London: C. Hurst, 1978); Ann Jefferson and David Robey, *Modern Literary Theory. A Comparative Introduction* (London: Batsford Academic and Educational Ltd, 1982).

III

Apart from their common method, the essays in this volume have a particular social location in common, namely the Society of Biblical Literature. Five of them were read in early versions as papers to meetings of the Society, and the other was written by invitation for a one-volume Bible commentary prepared under the auspices of the Society. In the dedication of this book I have mentioned the names of several members of the Society who are my regular partners in conversation, and to whom I owe a very great deal. Without an interpretative community of one's own, a community I can feel happy in, I mean, it is hard for me to imagine how good interpretative work can get done. I am very fortunate in having in my own department, and in the British Society for Old Testament Study, such communities; but the American Society of Biblical Literature is particularly challenging and creative, and I am immensely grateful for the opportunities its meetings have given me in the last few years for the explorations now contained in these pages.

There are three other essays that could have been included in this volume on the ground of their outlook and method, but which have appeared or will appear in other places. They are: 'Reading Esther from Left to Right', in which I attempt structuralist, feminist, materialist and deconstructionist readings of the book;[1] 'The Story of Michal in its Sequential

---

Among more specialized works I could mention Wolfgang Iser, *The Act of Reading. A Theory of Aesthetic Response* (Eng. tr.; Baltimore: Johns Hopkins Univerity Press, 1978); Hans Robert Jauss, *Toward an Aesthetic of Reception* (tr. Timothy Bahti; Brighton: The Harvester Press, 1982); Umberto Eco, *The Role of the Reader. Explorations in the Semiotics of Texts* (London: Hutchison & Co., 1981); and Robert C. Holub, *Reception Theory. A Critical Introduction* (London: Methuen, 1984).

1 'Reading Esther from Left to Right: Contemporary Strategies for Reading a Biblical Text', in *The Bible in Three Dimensions. Essays in Celebration of the Fortieth Anniversary of the Department of Biblical Studies, University of Sheffield*, ed. David J.A. Clines, Stephen E. Fowl and Stanley E. Porter (JSOTSup, 87; Sheffield: JSOT Press, 1990), pp. 31-52.

Unfolding' which undertakes a close reading of part of the David narrative;[1] and a collection of readings of the book of Job, feminist, vegetarian, materialist, and Christian.[2]

I conclude with a word of appreciation and thanks to Helen Orchard, my research assistant in 1989-90, whose painstaking and constructive contribution to the details of the book was indispensable in bringing it to a timely completion.

1 'The Story of Michal in its Sequential Unfolding', in David J.A. Clines and Tamara C. Eskenazi, *Michal, Wife of David: A Multi-voiced Telling of her Story* (Sheffield: JSOT Press, forthcoming).
2 In David J.A. Clines, *Job 1–20* (WBC, 17; Waco, Texas: Word Books, 1989), pp. xlvii-lvi; another version of this material has been published as 'Job', in *The Books of the Bible*, ed. B.W. Anderson (New York: Charles Scribner's Sons, 1989), pp. 181-201.

Chapter 1

WHAT DOES EVE DO TO HELP?
AND OTHER IRREDEEMABLY ANDROCENTRIC ORIENTATIONS
IN GENESIS 1–3*

Before feminism, everyone in the garden of Eden knew their place. At the top of the pyramid, even though the garden was not in Egypt, was God. Under him was his under-gardener Adam, created to carry on the maintenance of the garden that the master-gardener had planted. On the next rung down, the pyramid having mutated to a ladder, came Eve, who had not originally been thought of but had been created out of Adam as a 'helper' once all the animals had been paraded before Adam without a single helper being found among them. Beneath Eve were the animals, obviously unsatisfactory as helpers, but not in every respect inferior to her; for the cleverest of them has theological insight that Eve lacks.

This neat hierarchical system was not much disturbed by the first feminist visitors to the Garden of Eden, Elizabeth Cady Stanton and her fellow contributors to *The Woman's Bible* of 1895.[1] The narrative of Eve's creation, observed Stanton, 'makes her a mere afterthought [in creation]. The world in good running order without her. The only reason for her advent being the solitude of man'. Genesis 2 is nothing but an account of a 'petty surgical operation, to find material for

---

* The first version of this paper was read as a paper to the Rhetorical Criticism Section of the Society of Biblical Literature at its Annual Meeting in Boston, December 6, 1987. The theme of that section was "Women and Men and the Hebrew Bible'.
1 Elizabeth Cady Stanton, *The Woman's Bible: The Original Feminist Attack on the Bible* (Edinburgh: Polygon Books, 1985; abridgment of the original edition, New York: European Publishing Co., 1895, 1898).

the mother of the race'.[1] Things were quite different, indeed, for Stanton, in the creation narrative of ch. 1, where man and woman are created together: there woman is 'dignifie[d] as an important factor in the creation, equal in power and glory with man'. There, woman's creation is spoken of in the context of a sublime 'bringing order out of chaos; light out of darkness; giving each planet its place in the solar system; oceans and lands their limits'.[2] Now the contrast between the estimation of woman in the two creation narratives can only be explained as a deliberate subversion of the first by the second. 'It is evident', she comments, 'that some wily writer, seeing the perfect equality of man and woman in the first chapter, felt it important for the dignity and dominion of man to effect woman's subordination in some way'.[3]

The second wave of feminist criticism of the Hebrew Bible took a quite different direction. Since Phyllis Trible's epoch-making paper in the *Journal of the American Academy of Religion* for 1973, 'Depatriarchalizing in Biblical Interpretation',[4] the rank order in Eden has changed. Eve now stands on an equal footing with Adam, most feminist writers having accepted that Genesis 2–3, no less than Genesis 1, promotes the equality of the sexes.[5] 'Biblical religion is patriarchal', Trible averred, no question about it, and 'Hebrew literature', Genesis not excluded, 'comes from a male dominated society'. But 'the intentionality of biblical faith ... is neither to create nor to perpetuate patriarchy but rather to function as salvation for

---

1 Stanton, *The Woman's Bible*, p. 20.

2 Stanton, *The Woman's Bible*, p. 20.

3 Stanton, *The Woman's Bible*, p. 21.

4 Phyllis Trible, 'Depatriarchalizing in Biblical Interpretation', *JAAR* 41 (1973), pp. 30-48. The review of Trible's article by John W. Miller, 'Depatriarchalizing God in Biblical Interpretation: A Critique', *CBQ* 48 (1986), pp. 609-16, deals entirely with matters unrelated to the present essay.

5 Of the contrary opinion is Susan S. Lanser, '(Feminist) Criticism in the Garden: Inferring Genesis 2–3', in *Speech Act Theory and Biblical Criticism*, ed. Hugh C. White (Decatur, GA: Scholars Press, 1988) (= *Semeia* 41 [1988]), pp. 67-84 (68), writing that 'most contemporary feminist critics ... contend that by any reading Genesis 2–3 portrays man as primary and woman as subordinate'; but I do not know to whom she is referring.

both women and men', and 'the hermeneutical challenge' for
the contemporary critic is not to identify the sexism that is in
the Bible—presumably because that is too easy—, far less to
reject the Bible because of its sexism, but 'to translate biblical
faith without sexism'.[1]

Trible proceeded in her paper to bring to the surface a
number of places in Genesis 2–3 where, despite its overall
patriarchal or sexist orientation, sexism is, to use her term,
'disavowed'. She points, for example, to the Hebrew word
'ādām, usually translated 'man' or, as a personal name,
'Adam', and observes that it does not refer to the male, but is 'a
generic term for humankind'.[2] From this it follows that in the
command to *'ādām* in 2.16-17 not to eat of the tree of the
knowledge of good and evil, woman is as much addressed as
man, even though she has not at this point been created.
Secondly, she argues that the placement of the narrative of the
woman's creation at the end of the story does not signify that
woman is an afterthought; rather, since the last is so often in
Biblical literature first, the story means that the woman is the
culmination of creation.[3] Thirdly, she claims that the por-
trayals of the two characters Adam and Eve attribute, if anything, a greater intelligence and sensitivity to the woman.[4]
Fourthly, she maintains that the description of male
supremacy after Eden is represented by the narrative as
'perversions of creation', the woman having lost the freedom
and initiative with which she was created.[5] On such readings,
the Eden story crumbles as a prop for male chauvinism, and
becomes transformed into a text of liberating power.

1. Eve as 'Helper'

There remains a stumbling block in the text for the view that
Genesis 2–3 presents a picture of sexual equality. It is that the
woman's role is by design one of 'helper'. Even Phyllis Trible

---

1 Trible, 'Depatriarchalizing', p. 31.
2 Trible, 'Depatriarchalizing', p. 35.
3 Trible, 'Depatriarchalizing', p. 36.
4 Trible, 'Depatriarchalizing', p. 40: 'If the woman be intelligent,
  sensitive and ingenious, the man is passive, brutish, and inept'.
5 Trible, 'Depatriarchalizing', p. 41.

allows that 'the English word *helper* suggests an assistant, a subordinate, indeed, an inferior'. If the text is to be 'redeemed' from the androcentricity that makes the woman essentially a helper—and thus a subordinate—to the man, it must be that the text does not have the connotation we at first think it does.

The move to redeem the text proceeds by means of two arguments. The first is that *'ēzer*, 'helper', does not imply inferior rank, and the second is that *keneḡdô* 'corresponding to him', does in fact imply equal rank.

The first argument takes one of two forms. Either, it is claimed, as by Trible in her 1973 article, that since in some passages the term *'ēzer* is used of God as the helper of Israel, who creates and saves, the term cannot connote inferiority. She writes:

> *'ēzer* characterizes deity. God is the helper of Israel. As helper Yahweh creates and saves. Thus *'ēzer* is a relational term; it designates a beneficial relationship; and it pertains to God, people, and animals. By itself the word does not specify positions within relationships; more particularly, it does not imply inferiority ...[1]

Alternatively, it may be argued, as by Trible in her 1978 book, *God and the Rhetoric of Sexuality*,[2] that the frequent use of 'helper' for God has the result that in the Hebrew Bible the word 'helper' actually carries the connotation of 'superior'. Here she writes:

> [T]he English word *helper* suggests an assistant, a subordinate, indeed, an inferior, while the Hebrew word *'ēzer* carries no such connotation. To the contrary, in the Hebrew scriptures this word often describes God as the superior who creates and saves Israel. In our story the accompanying phrase, 'corresponding to it' (*keneḡdô*), tempers this connotation of superiority ...[3]

These two forms of the argument are not compatible, for either the term carries with it a connotation of rank or it does not. Either way, however, according to this argument, a

---

1 Trible, 'Depatriarchalizing', p. 36.
2 Phyllis Trible, *God and the Rhetoric of Sexuality* (Philadelphia: Fortress Press, 1978).
3 Trible, *God and the Rhetoric of Sexuality*, p. 90.

'helper' is not an inferior.

The second argument is, as Trible puts it, that the word *neged*, 'corresponding to', which is used alongside *'ēzer*, 'helper', connotes equality. Thus the two terms together mean that our text is speaking of 'a helper who is a counterpart', or, more precisely:

> the accompanying phrase, 'corresponding to it' (*kᵉnegdô*), tempers this connotation of superiority [implicit in 'helper'] to specify identity, mutuality, and equality.[1]

That being so, the woman is

> neither subordinate nor superior; [but] one who alleviates isolation through identity.[2]

I must admit that when I first read Phyllis Trible's account of 'helper' I immediately believed it, and went on doing so for more than a decade. I must further admit, in hindsight, that the reason why I believed it was because I wanted it to be true. I did not care to have a Bible that made women out to be inferior to men, and I was glad to find that a text which had so often been thought to mean that, even by feminists like Elizabeth Cady Stanton, did not have to be taken that way at all. I did not stop to ponder too long over the question how impressive feminist points like this could have become incorporated in a text that was by common consent patriarchal in its general intent. Perhaps I supposed that not even a patriarchal or sexist mindset can completely overwrite the commonsensical truth—as it seemed to me—that men and women are actually equal. But I should have realized that the contrast between the undenied 'patriarchy' of the Biblical literature and the claimed 'disavowal' of patriarchy in the same literature was actually something of an argument against Trible's interpretation.

A third-generation feminist—since feminists these days run though generations as fast as computers do—will no doubt be warmly appreciative of Phyllis Trible's success in putting such questions firmly on the hermeneutical agenda but at the same time eager to dissociate herself or himself

---

1 Trible, *God and the Rhetoric of Sexuality*, p. 90.
2 Trible, *God and the Rhetoric of Sexuality*, p. 90.

from any arguments that will not stand the cold light of day.

For myself, I must now question whether it is true that 'helper' does not imply inferiority. I cannot help (if the word will be allowed) feeling a certain sense of inferiority to everyone I help, and a sense of superiority to everyone who helps me. No doubt some professional 'helpers' have got into the unfortunate habit of regarding their clients, patients, and counsellees as in some way or other 'inferior' to them. But when I am myself the client or the patient, and visit my doctor, my psychiatrist or my social worker, I would like to believe that the best they can do is to *assist* me to be healthier or saner or more socially acceptable. Whether I am or not is not really in their gift, since for all their pills or nostrums what I am is 'down to me'—when it is not, as it used to be, 'up to me'. And when I help my student with an essay or my fellow motorist to change a wheel on the motorway, it is after all her essay or his tyre which she is writing or he is changing, and I am just, well, helping. Even if she could not get started without my help or he could not jack his car up without my jack, if I am 'helping' I am saying, This is not *my* task or *my* problem, but *yours*; neither is it *our* task or *our* problem on which we are co-operating together, it is *yours*. I am playing an 'inferior' role, even if in status I am superior. He has the right to decide to abandon the confounded car altogether and start hitching a lift; it is *his* car, and all I can do is help or not help. She has it within her power to decide to abandon the essay altogether and leave the university forthwith because essays are oppressive; I can only help or refuse to help with the essay. Women who have husbands who 'help' with the washing up know that 'helping' means: not taking responsibility but making it clear that washing up is women's work to which a man may descend out of chivalry or kindheartedness; helpers with washing up never do it right because they are just, well, helping.

The real question, however, I admit, is not what 'help' means in English, but what the verb *'āzar*, which we conventionally translate 'help', means in Hebrew, and what may be the meaning of nouns derived from it, like *'ōzer* 'helper' or *'ēzer* 'help', which is the word we have here in Genesis. What I conclude, from reviewing all the occurrences in the Hebrew Bible, is that though superiors may help inferiors, strong may help weak, gods may help humans, in the act of helping they are being 'inferior'. That is to say, they are subjecting themselves to a secondary, subordinate position. Their help may be necessary or crucial, but they are *assisting* some task that is already someone else's responsibility. They are not actually *doing* the task themselves, or even in cooperation, for there is different language for that.

Here are some examples. 1. When Joshua and the Israelites were besieging Lachish, the king of Gezer came up to 'help' the inhabitants of Lachish (Josh. 10.33). The Lachishites were presumably already doing all they could to resist the Israelites, and Horam of Gezer was merely adding his weight. He failed, incidentally, since 'Joshua smote him and his people, until he left none remaining'.

2. There is quite a lot of 'helping' going on in Biblical battles, of course. But it is always the outsider, the person whose fight it isn't, who is 'helping' those with the problem on their hands. The Syrians of Damascus come to 'help' the Syrians of Zobah against David in 2 Sam. 8.5; thirty-two kings are 'helping' Benhadad of Syria against Damascus (1 Kgs 20.16); chiefs of Manasseh 'helped' David against bands of raiders in 1 Chr. 12.21; Egypt's 'help' for Judah in rebellion against Assyria is worthless, according to Isaiah (30.7).

3. It is not really different with the gods. When Ahaz has been defeated by the Syrians (strange how Syrians figure so prominently in tales of helping), he decides that he will start sacrificing to the gods of Damascus, saying, 'Because the gods of the kings of Syria "helped" them, I will sacrifice to them that they may "help" me' (2 Chr. 28.23). To have gods 'helping' you in battle is not in principle different from having other kings 'help' you. It is *your* battle.

4. Can it then be different with *God* as a helper? When Jehoshaphat is in battle against the king of Syria (here come the Syrians again), he is mistaken for his ally Ahab of Israel. In surprise he 'cried out, and the LORD "helped" him. God drew them [the Syrians] away from him, for when [they] saw that it was not the king of Israel, they turned back from pursuing him' (2 Chr. 18.31-32). He needed the help, and it was help he could not have provided for himself; on the other hand, God did not take over the battle, by sending hailstones or

plagues, for example, to destroy the enemy, but merely gave some timely assistance. In fact, the help amounted solely to ensuring that the Syrians recognized when they got close enough to him that he was not their man.

5. Is it not very similar when psalmists aver that the Lord 'helped' them, or when they beg for his 'help'? One of them 'was pushed hard, so that I was falling, but the LORD "helped" me' (Ps. 118.13)—presumably to stand upright again. This sounds like a case of the Lord helping those who help themselves. People do not simply keel over when they are pushed; they instinctively try to righten themselves, but they can often do with a friendly helping hand. Or when psalmists call on the Lord to 'help' them (e.g. Ps. 30.10; 109.26), we are not to imagine they are idly sitting around doing nothing but waiting for God to deliver them from their distress. Being a helper of a psalmist does not make God live the psalmist's life for him, but to assist him in doing whatever the psalmist thinks he himself should be doing.

What has this to tell us about Eve? It persuades us, I should hope, that being a helper is not a Hebrew way of being an equal. Helping is the same the world over. Phyllis Trible was right when she affirmed that it is a 'relational' term that carried no implications about the respective statuses of the helper and the helpee. She was wrong, I think, when she argued that, because God is often said to be a 'helper', the term itself has acquired connotations of superiority. Whether the helper is a superior or not will depend entirely on other factors, extrinsic to the relationship constituted by the act of helping.

This general study of the term 'help' is, admittedly, perhaps not entirely adequate to establish the meaning of the word in the present context. How it functions here will no doubt only become truly transparent when we ask the question, So what does Eve *do* to help? She is created to be a helper, so where in the narrative do we see her actually helping? Is there anything that she does that will enable us to give content to the concept of 'helping'?

Now if we have only some vague notion of what she is expected to do to help, we shall not be surprised if nothing explicit is said in the narrative about her help. Suppose we agree with

S.R. Driver, Derek Kidner, or Phyllis Trible; then what 'helper' means will be:

> a *help*, who may in various ways assist him, and who may at the same time prove a companion, able to interchange thought with him, and be in other respects his intellectual equal.[1]

or

> the woman is presented wholly as [Adam's] partner and counterpart.[2.]

or

> a companion, one who is neither subordinate nor superior; one who alleviates isolation through identity.[3]

Such helping could be happening all the time but we would never hear of it in this narrative; it is too simple a text for subtleties like these to register. This sort of helping is surely not what this text has in mind.

What we are looking for is some task that Adam actually has to do which Eve helps him with. That is how helpers earn their keep. No one gets thanked for helping when all they have done is stand around being intellectually equal or alleviating people's isolation through identity—not when there is work to be done.

In the narrative, Adam has two tasks. The first is to till the garden and keep it (2.15). We never actually see Adam tilling the ground, so we cannot tell for sure whether Eve has been lending him a hand. But since nothing in the narrative says it, we doubt it; and we are confirmed in our doubt by the divine sentences against the two of them in 3.16-19. For there, while Adam is sentenced for his guilt to sweat over his work on the land and to struggle with thorns and thistles, Eve is not. That is not her sphere. She is inside having children while Adam is out there sweating and struggling with the soil. She has been no help on that front, we conclude.

---

1 S.R. Driver, *The Book of Genesis* (London: Methuen, 12th edn, 1926), p. 41.
2 D. Kidner, *Genesis. An Introduction and Commentary* (TOTC; London: Tyndale Press, 1967), p. 65.
3 Trible, *God and the Rhetoric of Sexuality*, p. 90.

Adam's second task is to name the animals. This requires imagination, even if you already speak Hebrew. We might have thought that this was where Eve could be expected to lend a hand. Not physically demanding work, but being intellectually equal and capable of interchanging thought with Adam would seem to be a recommendation for the job. Unfortunately, Adam has completely finished this task, and given names to all the cattle, and to the birds of the air and to every beast of the field, before Eve ever appears on the scene (2.20). Eve is no help here either.[1]

Let us approach the question by asking, Well, what does Eve actually *do*, and is *that* a help? That way we very quickly find that there is nothing that Eve actually *does* inside the garden except have the conversation with the snake and eat the forbidden fruit. It does not take a great deal of acumen to recognize that having theological conversations with snakes it not a great help, not if you have any ambition to stay in the garden and keep it under control for the owner to take evening walks in without seeing the work pile up. Not many people, incidentally, have given much thought to what happens to God's evenings in the garden after he has had to sack the gardener.

We conclude that either Eve is no help at all, or else we have been looking in the wrong direction. What is it that Adam needs Eve's help for? Only to fulfil a divine command that we have been forgetting about! In 1.28 God has said, 'Be fruitful and multiply, and fill the earth'.[2] This is something Adam finds

---

1 Mark Twain of course twists the story, to amusing effect. His Adam complains: 'I get no chance to name anything myself. The new creature names everything that comes along, before I can get in a protest. And always that same pretext is offered—it *looks* like the thing. There is the dodo, for instance. Says the moment one looks at it one sees at a glance that it "looks like a dodo". It will have to keep that name, no doubt. It wearies me to fret about it, and it does no good anyway ... The naming goes recklessly on, in spite of anything I can do' (*Extracts from Adam's Diary* [New York: Harper and Brothers, 1906], pp. 5, 11). Let it be noted, lest Twain be thought a misogynist, that *Eve's Diary* deconstructs Adam's.

2 Cf. Phyllis A. Bird, arguing that the sexual distinction in 1.28 relates entirely to procreation; 'sexual constitution', she writes, 'is the presupposition of the blessing of increase' ("'Male and Female He Created Them': Gen 1:27b in the Context of the Priestly Account

he is unable to manage by himself. Only with an Eve can Adam multiply. This reading explains the narrative more convincingly than any other understanding of 'helper'. From this viewpoint, the Lord says that 'it is not good that the man should be alone' not because Adam is lonely or has no lively intellectual conversation when he comes in from the garden at nights but because he will have no chance at all of filling the earth so long as there is only one of him. The Lord brings the animals to Adam 'to see what he would call them' not because the Lord has run out of ideas for names, but in the hope that Adam will recognize a mate. Adam doesn't, of course, and makes it very plain when he calls a camel a camel that he doesn't regard it as a she-Adam. Camels are all very well, and they can be a great help. But when it comes to the purpose God has in mind, camels are no help at all. As the narrative says, 'But for the man there was not found a helper fit for him' (2.20). When he does see Eve, he recognizes her as a mate, and says, with unmistakable relief, 'This *at last* is bone of my bone', which is to say, the same sort of creature as myself, and he promptly names her *'iššâ*, a female *'îš*—which is to say, a *woman*, a female *man*. He can begin to see his way clear to filling the earth with progeny.

This view of Eve's helpfulness also explains the narrative's emphasis on nakedness, on the man cleaving to the woman, and on their being one flesh (2.23-25). It is also clear that God regards Eve as primarily a child-bearing creature: he has not said that it is not good *for Adam* that he should be alone, but that it is not good at all; he is not thinking so much of Adam as of himself and of his designs for the human race. And after the sin of the couple he does not punish the woman by threatening her with demotion to intellectual inferiority or by rendering her incapable of keeping up interesting conversation with her partner, but he most severely punishes her by promising to make the one thing she has been created to do difficult for her: 'I will greatly multiply your pain in childbearing; in pain you shall bring forth children' (3.16). Just as Adam will find his work as farmer painful, so she will find hers as mother. Nor will either of them have much choice about opting out of their role. He will have to sweat because they both must eat; she will have to suffer the pain of childbirth over and over again because, as 3.16b puts it, she will keep on wanting her husband to make love to her and he will insist on doing so anyway; despite the pregnancies that will inevitably result and the pain of childbirth that will surely follow, her desire will be for her husband, and he will keep on being dominating. Both of them will be locked into inescapable cycles of pain, but together they will nevertheless be fulfilling the divine programme. Adam sees the point very exactly when immediately after the divine sentences on the two of them he calls her name Eve, 'life', 'because she was the mother of all living' (3.20). She has not yet had a child, and is not yet the mother of anyone; but her function is as plain as her two names: Ishshah-Eve, or, as we would say, Woman-Life, exists for the procreation of children. That is what Eve does to help.

So the Fathers were right after all. Not the rabbis who argued that the reason why it was not good for the man to be alone was in case people should say that Adam was as important as God, both of them being one and all alone (so e.g. Rashi on 2.18[1]). Augustine spoke for the fathers of the Christian church when he candidly remarked that a male companion would have been better for society and enjoyment. He could not

> think of any reason for woman's being made as man's helper if we dismiss the reason of procreation ... [She] was of small intelligence and ... lives more in accordance with the promptings of the inferior flesh than by the superior reason.[2]

And he put our point exactly:

---

1 'So that they should not say there are two Rulers: the Almighty is One in the Heavens above, and he has no participant, and this one [Adam] is one of Earth, and he [also] has no partner' (James H. Lowe, *'Rashi' on the Pentateuch. Genesis* [London: The Hebrew Compendium Publishing Company, 1928], p. 57 (my punctuation).

2 Augustine, *De Genesi ad litteram libri duodecim* 9.5.9 (J.-P. Migne, *Patrologia Cursus Completus [Patrologia Latina]*, vol. 34 [Paris, 1845], col. 396 (= Corpus Scriptorum Ecclesiasticorum Latinorum 28/1); English translation by John Hammon, S.J., *St. Augustine, The Literal Meaning of Genesis* (Ancient Christian Writers, 41-42; Ramsey, NJ: Paulist, 1982).

But if the woman was not made for the man as a helper in begetting children, for what purpose was she created as a helper? She was not to till the soil with him since there was not yet any such toil to make help necessary. If there were such a need, a male helper would have been preferable. The same thing could be said of the comfort of another's presence if, perhaps, Adam wearied of solitude. How much more agreeable for companionship in a life shared together would be two male friends rather than a man and a woman.[1]

Aquinas likewise believed that

It was absolutely necessary to make woman ... as a help for man; not, indeed, to help him in any other work, as some have maintained, because where most work is concerned man can get help more conveniently from another man than from a woman; but to help him in the work of procreation.[2]

The outcome is that the text persists in its its androcentric orientation, from which it cannot be redeemed, despite the constructive programme of second-generation feminists among Biblical scholars. We readers for our part cannot accept that procreation is the sole or even the primary purpose of women, and if that is what the text says we cannot accept the text. That is to say, a feminist critique raises, as it does so often, the question of Biblical authority.

2. *The Naming of Eve*

Once we have recognized that on this crucial matter the Genesis narrative is thoroughly androcentric—which is no more than we should have suspected anyway—the way is

---

1 Augustine, *De Genesi ad litteram libri duodecim* 9.5.9. See most recently Susan E. Schreiner, 'Eve, the Mother of History. Reaching for the Reality of History in Augustine's Later Exegesis of Genesis', in Gregory A. Robbins, *Genesis 1–3 in the History of Exegesis. Intrigue in the Garden* (Studies in Women and Religion, 27; Lewiston, NY: Edwin Mellen, 1988), pp. 135-86, and, more generally, John A. Phillips, *Eve: The History of an Idea* (San Francisco: Harper and Row, 1984).

2 Aquinas, *Summa Theologiae* Part Ia, Q. 92, art. 1; translation from St Thomas Aquinas, *Summa Theologiae. Latin text and English translation*, vol. 13, ed. Edmund Hill (London: Blackfriars in conjunction with Eyre and Spottiswoode, 1964), pp. 34-35.

clear for identifying other points in the narrative that manifest the same orientation.

An obvious case is the naming of Eve (2.25; 3.20). It has been
customary to observe, as G. von Rad does, for example, that
'name-giving in the ancient Orient was primarily an exercise
of sovereignty, of command'.[1] Feminist interpreters also allow
that such is indeed the significance of the naming of the
animals,[2] but have sometimes argued that the so-called
naming of Eve in 2.25 is no such thing. Thus Trible suggests
that since neither the verb nor the noun 'name' is in the text,
but only the verb 'call', there is no naming here and so no
authority of the man over the woman.[3] Now it is no doubt true
that in other places in Genesis 2–11 the naming formula is 'X
called his *name* Y' (4.25, 26; cf. 4.17), but what is also true—
and what Trible does not point out—is that in Genesis 1 all the
naming has gone on exclusively by means of the verb 'call',
without the word 'name' ever being used.[4] So it cannot be
denied that 'calling' is a perfectly acceptable Hebrew way of
describing naming; and it is hard to see why the writer of
Genesis 2, even if a different person from the author of Genesis
1, should have thought otherwise.[5] Moreover, it would be necessary to explain what 'calling' someone 'woman' could mean
if it does not mean calling her *by that name*. Trible argues that
''*Adham* recognizes sexuality by the words *'ishshah* and *'ish*'.[6]
But that could only be true if an adjective, not a noun, were

---

1 G. von Rad, *Genesis. A Commentary* (OTL; revised edn; Philadelphia: Westminster, 1972), p. 83.
2 Trible, 'Depatriarchalizing', p. 36: ''*Adham* names them and
   thereby exercises power over them'; similarly Trible, *God and the
   Rhetoric of Sexuality*, p. 97.
3 Trible, 'Depatriarchalizing', p. 38.
4 See also the thorough analysis of the terminology for name-giving,
   by George W. Ramsey, 'Is Name-Giving an Act of Domination in
   Genesis 2:23 and Elsewhere?', *CBQ* 50 (1988), pp. 24-35.
5 See also Lanser, '(Feminist) Criticism in the Garden', p. 73, observing from the standpoint of speech-act theory that '[h]aving set up
   the sequence in which *hā'ādām* is authorized to name [i.e. 2.19-22],
   the text has already generated the context in which "call" may be
   inferred to mean "call the name of", despite the abbreviated surface
   form'.
6 Trible, 'Depatriarchalizing', p. 38.

used; if he called her 'female' because she was taken out of 'male', there might well be no *naming*. Calling someone 'great' or 'cowardly' would not be naming; but calling them 'king' or 'mother' authorizes the use of that term as a *name*. 'Woman' here can only be a name, and it makes no odds that 'woman' is a common noun, not a proper name, as Trible objects.

Things are no different when Adam 'call[s] his wife's name Eve' in 3.20. There is no hint in the text that 'the naming itself faults the man for corrupting a relationship of mutuality and equality', as Trible claims.[1] One may agree rather with von Rad that

> One must see the man's naming of the woman as an act of faith, certainly not faith in promises that lie hidden, veiled in the penalties, but rather an embracing of life, which as a great miracle and mystery is maintained and carried by the motherhood of woman over hardship and death.[2]

The naming of the woman by the man, on both occasions, I conclude, signifies his authority over her.[3] She does not name him, she does not designate his function. The man's point of view is the same as God's, which is the same as the narrator's:

---

1 Trible, 'Depatriarchalizing', p. 41.
2 Von Rad, *Genesis*, p. 96. Cf. C. Westermann, *Genesis 1–11. A Commentary* (tr. John J. Scullion; Minneapolis: Augsburg, 1984), p. 268: 'The blessing conferred on humans, namely the power of procreation, has not been lost by the crime and the punishment'.
3 Ramsey, 'Is Name-Giving an Act of Domination?', pp. 34-35, resists such a conclusion, arguing that name-giving is an act of *discernment* of the true nature or essence of the one or the thing named rather than of *domination*. There is, however, no reason why *discernment* and *domination* should be regarded as mutually exclusive; the fact remains that it is Adam who names Eve, and not the other way about. Coincidentally I find in my files a clipping of a newspaper article by the columnist Jill Tweedie, entitled 'The power of the namer over the named'. She writes: 'Ted Hughes, Poet Laureate and erstwhile husband of the poet Sylvia Plath, is once more plagued by Plathites and forced to defend, among other things, his choice of the name "Sylvia Plath Hughes" for her gravestone ... [T]he right to name is the right to exercise a half-magical, half-brutal power over the one named. To name is to possess, always has been, always will be. If I name you, you are mine. If you name me, I am yours' (*The Independent*, April 24, 1989).

in 2.25 woman is formed of Adam's substance and is consequently like him, as the animals are not; her name Woman
signals the similarity between them. In 3.20 Woman's function as childbearer is denoted by her name Life, Eve. In both
cases the man understands her identity and her function, and
has the authority to pronounce upon them. The orientation is
unambiguously androcentric.

3. *The Term* 'ādām

A further sign of the male-centredness of Genesis 2–3 is the
usage of the terms for 'man' and 'humankind'. It is a male
that is created first, and he is called 'ādām, 'human'. This is
not because until the creation of woman the 'earth-creature'
is sexually undifferentiated,[1] but because the male is most
naturally thought of, in the horizon of this text, as the obvious
representative of humanity.[2] Hebrew is no different from
what English has been on this score until quite recently: the
ordinary word for 'human' (*man*) has been a word for 'male'
but not for 'female' even though females are human.

It is true that once the woman has been created the more
explicitly sexually differentiated language is used: he is 'îš in
counterpoint to her being 'iššâ: the 'îš leaves his father and
mother and cleaves to his 'iššâ (2.24), the 'iššâ gives some of
the fruit to her 'îš (3.6). But this is not a differentiation that
persists: in 3.9 Yahweh God is calling to the 'ādām, in 3.12 the
'ādām is speaking, in 3.20 the 'ādām is naming his 'iššâ. In the

---

1 Trible, *God and the Rhetoric of Sexuality*, p. 98.
2 See further, Lanser, '(Feminist) Criticism in the Garden', p. 72,
 arguing, on the basis of speech-act theory (that meaning is constituted not just by words and sentences but by the total context of the
 act of speech), that the context implies the identification of the
 'ādām as male. '[W]hen a being assumed to be human is introduced into a narrative, that being is also assumed to have sexual as
 well as grammatical gender. The masculine form of *hā'ādām* and
 its associated pronouns will, by inference, define *hā'ādām* as male.
 I am not suggesting that one *cannot* read *hā'ādām* as a sex-neutral
 figure; I am saying that readers *will* not ordinarily read Genesis 2
 in this way. Gendered humans are the unmarked case; it is not
 hā'ādām's maleness that would have to be marked but the *absence*
 of maleness.'

perspective of the text, it is the male that is naturally and properly *'ādām*, human; the female is never called *'ādām*, nor is *'ādām* even used as a collective noun to include both the man and the woman. This is no more than we would expect from any narrative in the Hebrew Bible, simple and mindless androcentricity.

4. *Male and Female in Genesis 1*

Can this androcentricity also be identified in Genesis 1? Feminist critics since the days of Elizabeth Cady Stanton have been unanimous that it cannot. Stanton herself found that in Genesis 1 woman is 'dignifie[d] as an important factor in the creation, equal in power and glory with man'. Her creation is spoken of in the context of a sublime 'bringing order out of chaos; light out of darkness; giving each planet its place in the solar system; oceans and lands their limits'.[1]

It is rare to find a feminist writer expressing any doubt over the equality of the sexes in Genesis 1. Phyllis Bird, however, I observed, wrote an interesting footnote:

> The P formulation [of Gen. 1.26-27] implies an essential equality of the two sexes. But its implications were only partially perceived by the priestly writer, whose own culturally determined ideas concerning appropriate roles and activities of men and women generally fail to reflect this insight. Thus male genealogies and an exclusively male priesthood dominate the rest of his work.[2]

This, it must be said, is a self-deconstructing footnote. For if the unmistakable tendency of the author is androcentric, and if in our text he says nothing explicit about the equality of the sexes, but can only be claimed to 'imply' things which he himself 'only partially perceive[s]', what grounds can there be for supposing that these things are in fact even 'implied'? In a later,

1 Stanton, *The Woman's Bible*, p. 20.
2 Phyllis Bird, 'Images of Women in the Old Testament', in *The Bible and Human Liberation. Political and Social Hermeneutics*, ed. Norman K. Gottwald (Maryknoll, NY: Orbis, 1983), pp. 252-88 (287) (originally published in *Religion and Sexism: Images of Women in the Jewish and Christian Traditions*, ed. Rosemary Radford Ruether [New York: Simon & Schuster, 1974], pp. 41-88).

and more thoroughly exegetical, article Phyllis Bird in fact drew back from the affirmation of the equality of the sexes for the author of Genesis 1 and spoke of removing 'the incongruous portrait of P as an equal-rights theologian' and reading Genesis 1 in harmony with the androcentric outlook of the P writing as a whole.[1] Hers, however, has been something of a lone voice among feministically inclined interpreters of Genesis in recent decades.

Such preliminary considerations will in any case not preclude an examination of the text itself. It begins:

> Let us make *'ādām* as[2] our image after our likeness,
> and let them rule (*yirdû*) over the fish and the birds ... (1.26).

Why is *yirdû* plural? Not because *'ādām* is to be made as male and female, for that has not yet been said, but because *'ādām* is a collective noun, referring to the human race as a whole, just as the collectives *dag* and *'ôp* refer to birds and fish in general in the same verse. It is humanity at large that is here envisaged as about to be created, just as it is the great sea monsters (*tannînim gedōlîm*) that are envisaged in 1.21. Let us be clear: females are not excluded from the content of *'ādām* here, because—and only because—so far as we know, Hebrew speakers never thought women were not human. But neither are they specifically in view. The text does not mean to say that women, every bit as much as men, are to have dominion over the animals—not so much because women are not equal with men, though we know in advance that from the text's perspective they most probably are *not*—but because it is undifferentiated humanity that is being spoken of.[3] It is not that the

---

1 Phyllis A. Bird, '"Male and Female He Created Them": Gen 1:27b in the Context of the Priestly Account of Creation', *HTR* 74 (1981), pp. 129-59 (156).
2 On the translation, see David J.A. Clines, 'The Image of God in Man', *Tyndale Bulletin* 19 (1968), pp. 53-103 (96).
3 Similarly too Bird, '"Male and Female He Created Them"': 'There is no message of shared dominion here, no word about the distribution of roles, responsibility, and authority between the sexes, no word of sexual equality. What is described is a task for the species (*kibšūhā*) and the position of the species in relation to the other orders of creatures (*rĕdû*). The social metaphors to which the key verbs point are male, derived from male experience and models,

text denies the authority of women over the animal creation; it is simply that it ignores women as women, just as it ignores men as men—however much it implicitly adopts a male perspective.

The same is surely the case when the creation of humanity as the image of God is being spoken of. The text is quite explicit:

> And God created *'ādām* as his image,
> as the image of God he created *'ōtô* (*'ādām* collectively) (1.27).

The singular *'ōtô* shows that *'ādām* is being used as a collective. Whether what is true of undifferentiated humanity is true of all individual humans is a question that has to be solved on its own merits, and the answer cannot be automatically assumed. It might be that it is humanity as a species that is the image of God, or it might be that every individual human being is personally the image of God. Nothing in the wording makes this clear.

When we turn to the third clause of 1.27,

> male and female he created them (*'ōtām*),

there is nothing in the present text that has anticipated this element. There has been no suggestion, for example, that it is in the existence of male and female that the image of God will consist,[1] for the conceptualization male-female has not been present when the idea of the image of God has been introduced in v. 26. And in any case it seems evident that being in the image of God is to be related, if anything, to humankind's having rule over the animals.

Where does the specification male-female arise from, then? It can only be by correspondence with the report of the creation of other living creatures that they are created 'according to their kind' (1.21 [*bis*], 24 [*bis*], 25 [*ter*]). The 'kinds' according to which humanity is created are: male and female. That is the most obvious and pervasive line of discrimination among

---

the dominant social models of patriarchal society' (p. 151).
1 See, for example, Karl Barth, *Church Dogmatics* 3/1 (E.Tr. Edinburgh: T. and T. Clark, 1958), pp. 194-95; on which see also F. Horst, 'Face to Face: The Biblical Doctrine of the Image of God', *Interp* 4 (1950), pp. 259-70; Clines, 'The Image of God in Man', pp. 92ff.; Bird, '"Male and Female He Created Them"', pp. 132-33.

members of the human race: male and female are the 'kinds' of humans there are.

What does not follow from this is that in the view of Genesis 1 men and women are equal. Not at least in general. They are equal in some respects; for example, they are equally created by God. So too are great sea monsters (1.21). They are equally human, both male and female being included in the term '*ādām*. But that does not mean that as humans they are equal. They are equal in being blessed by God, though that does not necessarily mean that they are blessed to the same extent or in the same way; the living creatures of the sea and the birds are also 'blessed' by God (1.22), as is also the sabbath day (2.3). But none of this amounts to a doctrine or theory of an equality of the sexes. Most of the time the distinction between the sexes is not in view; it is humanity at large that is created, created in the image of God, blessed, told to be fruitful, to fill the earth and subdue it, and rule over the animals. To say, for example, that women as well as men are created as the image of God is to move beyond the horizon of the text.

The most that we could say is that Genesis 1 itself does not exclude the idea of the equality of the sexes. The question then arises, however, whether or for how long we may consider Genesis 1 'in itself'. For Genesis 1 lies very definitely in a context constituted by what immediately follows, a narrative that tells a similar tale, of the creation of humans. And that context of Genesis 1 excludes the idea of the equality of the sexes, quite categorically. For the context shows that while the woman is fully human, she is definitely subordinate to the man.[1] And if, on the other hand, it is insisted that the context of Genesis 1

---

1 Phyllis Bird reads the evidence differently, arguing that in the Yahwistic account of creation 'the primary meaning of sexuality is seen in psycho-social, rather than biological, terms ... The intended partnership implies a partnership of equals, characterized by mutuality of attraction, support and commitment' ('"Male and Female He Created Them"', p. 158). This view is based, however, on some inferences from the narrative, especially that of Gen. 2.23, rather than on the explicit terming of the woman a 'helper'. And contrariwise, Susan Lanser finds in Genesis 1 a 'theologically egalitarian impulse manifested more openly' than in what is for her the evidently subordinationist perspective of Genesis 2–3; cf. '(Feminist) Criticism in the Garden', p. 79.

must be taken to be, not the text that is contiguous with it in the present form of the book, but the text which which it apparently once cohered, the supposed 'priestly writing', the answer is no different. For the absence of any repetition of the idea of the equality of the sexes from the rest of the priestly work effectively eliminates it from consideration here. For the priestly writing is well known as estimating men and women differently, and as having moreover the figures to prove it: for example, as a dedicatee to religious service an adult male is worth 50 silver shekels, a female 30; a male minor is worth 20 shekels, a female 10; a male child is worth 5 shekels, a female 3; an elderly male is worth 15, a female 10 (Lev. 27.2-8). Females are thus worth between 50% and 66% what males are worth. Women, in other words, are not worthless or negligible, but they are not equal to men. If the priestly writing rather than Genesis 2–3 is to be taken as the context of Genesis 1, the androcentricity of Leviticus must, even if there were no other explicit statement,[1] be our yardstick for interpreting Genesis 1.

The outcome is that Genesis 1 also is indefeasibly androcentric. No more than Genesis 2–3 can it be 'redeemed' from its patriarchal or sexist stance.[2]

5. *Eve and the 'Authority' of the Bible*

A feminist critique, as we have seen, directly raises the question of Biblical authority. If I am right in my understanding of the text, the text is in conflict with a principle that is not a passing fashion of the modern world, but has become a fundamental way of looking at the world. It is not only people who

1 Among other elements of the 'priestly work' that display the same orientation may be mentioned the presumption of legitimacy through descent from males, the absence of women from the performance of the cult, and the covenantal sign of circumcision that is relevant only to males (cf. Bird, '"Male and Female he Created Them"', p. 156).

2 Cf. the recent observations of Phyllis A. Bird on certain practical questions in translating the sexist language of the Old Testament: 'Translating Sexist Language as a Theological and Cultural Problem', *USQR* 42 (1988), pp. 89-95.

would call themselves feminists who want to insist that
women are fully human, in every sense that men are, that the
issue of the equality of the sexes is not a joke but something we
really have to get right if we want to be serious people. What is
more, feminist principles are, for many of us, not some godless
philosophy wished upon us by the spirit of the age, but an
application of the Christian gospel. The equality of the sexes is
a cause explicitly promoted by the Christian teaching that 'in
Christ ... there is neither male nor female' (Gal. 3.28) It is not a
principle that I for my part can give up, not even for the Bible's
sake, if that is what it is, without a loss of personal integrity.[1]

What shall I do with Genesis, then? One of my options is to
ascribe the sexism of the text to the primitive world of the Old
Testament, and sigh my relief that in New Testament
Christianity we do these things much better. I then deal with
the problem of the authority of the Old Testament by denying
that it has any. The difficulty remains that the world of the
New Testament is not so different, not if a letter ascribed to
Paul can insist that in church a woman should 'learn in
silence with all submissiveness'; she is not to 'teach or have
authority over men' because 'Adam was formed first, then
Eve; and Adam was not deceived, but the woman was deceived
and became a transgressor'. Our New Testament author has
read his Genesis well when he goes on to allow, 'Yet woman
will be saved through bearing children, if she continues in
faith and love and holiness, with modesty' (1 Tim. 2.11-15).
Child-bearing is her proper function, and let her not get
involved in seminars with snakes.

A second option is to accept the authority of the Bible in
matters to which the heart and mind can gladly give consent,

1 Cf. Letty M. Russell, 'Authority and the Challenge of Feminist
  Interpretation', in *Feminist Interpretation of the Bible* (Oxford:
  Blackwell, 1985), pp. 137-49. She begins her article: 'Feminists of
  the Jewish and Christian faiths are faced with a basic dilemma.
  Are they to be faithful to the teachings of the Hebrew scriptures and
  the Christian scriptures, or are they to be faithful to their own
  integrity as whole human beings? ... [T]his issue ... is pressed upon
  [feminists] every time they propose an interpretation or perspective
  that challenges a dominant view of scriptural authority and interpretation' (p. 137).

and to reject it when it conflicts, not with our prejudices but, with our deeply held convictions. This may be scandalous to purists, who cannot imagine the authority of the Bible being anything other than total, and equal in every part; but it sounds like a reasonable compromise of the kind that actual living tends to be made up from. Here is Letty Russell's statement of this option in her essay in the volume she edited under the title *Feminist Interpretation of the Bible*:

> In spite of the patriarchal nature of the Biblical texts, I myself have no intention of giving up the biblical basis of my theology. With Rosemary Ruether I would argue that the Bible has a critical or liberating tradition embodied in its 'prophetic-messianic' message of continuing self-critique. The evidence for a biblical message of liberation for women, as for other marginalized groups, is not found just in particular stories about women or particular female images of God. It is found in God's intention for the mending of all creation. The Bible has authority in my life because it makes sense of my experience and speaks to me about the meaning and purpose of my humanity in Jesus Christ. In spite of its ancient and patriarchal worldviews, in spite of its inconsistencies and mixed messages, the story of God's love affair with the world leads me to a vision of New Creation that impels my life ... For me the Bible is 'scripture', or sacred writing, because it functions as 'script', or prompting for life.[1]

In spite of what is, to my taste, a certain sentimentality in the language, I like that statement well enough. There is just one thing I would query, and it is at this point that I think my view could be taken as a third option for the issue of the authority of the Bible. My question is, Why then go on talking about the *authority* of the Bible?

Does not the very concept of 'authority' come from a world we have (thankfully) left behind? To imagine that the Bible could be 'authoritative' sounds as if we still are wanting to plunder it for prooftexts for theological warfare. As if one sentence from the immense unsystematic collection of literature that is the Bible could *prove* anything. As if truth in matters of

---

1 Russell, 'Authority and the Challenge of Feminist Interpretation', p. 138.

religion could be arrived at by a process like that of the medi-
aeval academic disputation. As if texts mattered more than
people.

Letty Russell herself has great difficulty with the concept of
'authority', though she herself does not know it or does not
acknowledge it. What she wants to say about the Bible is that it
is the basis of her theology, that it has one 'liberating' tradition
in it (presumably among other non-liberating traditions) that
she welcomes, and that it makes sense of her experience and
'speaks to [her] about the meaning of [her] humanity', that it
leads her to a vision that impels her life, and functions as
prompting for life. None of this sounds to me in the least like
authority. Here there is not a lot of No Parking, Write on one
side of the paper only, Queue here, Do not collect £200.

So why not say, Authority is not the point. The authority of a
text has to do with its nature; we want to be saying things
about the Bible that have to do with its *function*. We want to be
saying, not so much that the Bible is right, not even that the
Bible is wrong, but that it impacts for good upon people. Despite
everything, we might want to add, despite its handicaps,
despite the fact that it has misled people and promoted patriarchy, it has an unquenchable capacity—when taken in conjunction with a commitment to personal integrity—to inspire
people, bring out the best in them and suggest a vision they
could never have dreamed of for themselves. Think of it as
dogma and you will at times, as over the matter of men and
women, either be wrong or get it wrong. Think of it rather as a
resource for living which has no authority but which nevertheless manages to impose itself powerfully upon people.
Strange in a way that feminists have not yet seen that
'authority' is a concept from the male world of power-
relations, and that a more inclusive human language of
influence, encouragement and inspiration would be more
acceptable to everyone and more likely to win the assent of
minds as well as hearts.

Chapter 2

WHAT HAPPENS IN GENESIS*

What happens in Genesis? Genesis looks like a narrative book, with events being told in roughly chronological order and characters remaining reasonably recognizable throughout their appearances. So it is a proper question, when opening the book, to ask, What happens in this narrative? That is to say, plot is the subject of this enquiry. Of the author or sources of Genesis I confess (or allege, it is the same thing) that I know nothing, and so I assume nothing. But, like most readers everywhere, I expect narratives to have plots. Only after I have tried hard to discern a plot, and failed, will I decide that this book as a whole is no plotted story, but merely a chronicle or merely some incoherent collection of episodes.

But if I go looking for plot in Genesis, is there not perhaps a danger of inventing a plot where none exists? A possibility, perhaps, but not a danger. I have decided not to wince at the

* The first version of this Chapter was read as a paper to the Society of Biblical Literature, International Meeting, Heidelberg, August 10, 1987. Some parts of the paper in its present form, especially the footnotes and a number of the observations on the Jacob story, are the work of my former PhD student, Laurence A. Turner, whose thesis, *Announcements of Plot in Genesis*, will be published in the JSOT Supplement Series in 1990. Since the ideas in the present paper were discussed over many months by both of us, it is impossible now to identify their origin entirely fairly; I can only acknowledge with thanks the many stimulating conversations with Dr Turner which enabled my own thoughts to develop further. The reader will find in the monograph referred to a much more thoroughgoing treatment of points sketched in this paper and many other original observations besides. See also his 'Lot as Jekyll and Hyde", in *The Bible in Three Dimensions. Essays in Celebration of Forty Years of Biblical Studies in the University of Sheffield*, ed. David J.A. Clines, Stephen E. Fowl and Stanley E. Porter (JSOTSup, 87; Sheffield: JSOT Press, 1990), pp. 85-98.

possibility of being caught out in the act of thinking something about a work that its author never thought. If such boldness may be forgiven, I would even ask, What could be a more appreciative reading of a text than to find a coherence never before discerned, not even by its original author? It is being seen these days more clearly than ever before that we readers always have a goodly share in creating meaning out of texts—though not, if we are wise, arbitrarily or individualistically or completely subjectively. The words on the page are an objective reality that we must always measure up to, take account of, fall in with. But they do not wear their meanings or the way they hang together—their coherence—on their face or on their sleeve. Making meaning, making sense, making coherence, is our task, not theirs.

Texts of course do not always leave everything up to the reader; they have ways of dropping clues about plot or meaning. This text of Genesis uses three such ways at least. One is the Headline. 'After these things God tested Abraham' (22.1) signals how we are to read the story of the near-sacrifice of Isaac, not as a Hitchcockian suspense thriller, nor as one of Phyllis Trible's texts of terror, nor as an aetiological legend, but as a test of Abraham's reflexes—not just whether he will obey the insane command to slaughter the promised son, but also whether he will be ready to stay his hand when a voice from the sky announces that the previous command is now inoperative.

Second is the Punchline, as when Joseph tells his brothers in 45.8 that it was not they but God who sent him into Egypt, or in 50.20 that while they were devising an evil plot against him, God was devising a plot of blessing for the ancestral family and many others. Another punchline was 3.24 where we learned only in the very last phrase of the Eden story what the purpose of the expulsion was: to guard the way to the tree of life.

Third among the text's clues to plot is the Announcement of how the story may be expected to develop. The Announcements may in principle be made by the narrator or by the characters, but in Genesis they are all put in the mouths of characters in the narrative. They take the form of a divine command or prediction, a father's birth oracle, and a boyhood dream. They contain either a reversal of the prevailing situation or an inversion of what might reasonably be expected. So in ch. 1 the Announcement is that the human species are to be fruitful and multiply and also to 'subdue' the earth and take the mastery over the animals. In ch. 12 it is that a childless octogenarian will become the father of many descendants. In ch. 25 it is that the elder son will be servant to the younger. In ch. 37 it is that the second-youngest son is to be lord over his eleven brothers and his parents.

I shall be concentrating on these four Announcements in this quest for plot, asking, Do things turn out as the Announcement leads us to believe? And if not, In what way not? These are indeed not entirely novel questions to ask, but no one seems previously to have identified these Announcements as markers against which the development of the plot of Genesis is to be measured.[1]

---

1 Others have indeed noted from time to time the programmatic nature of the texts we have identified as 'Announcements'. On 1.28 Walter Brueggemann, 'The Kerygma of the Priestly Writers', *ZAW* 84 (1972), pp. 397-414 (400), suggests that 'the formidable blessing declaration of Gen 12.8 provides a focus for understanding the kerygma of the entire tradition'. However, Brueggemann limits his discussion to the so-called P tradition. On 12.1-3, John C.L. Gibson, *Genesis* (DSB; Edinburgh: Saint Andrew Press, 1982), vol. 2, p. 12, comments: 'Everything he does following his call and everything that happens to him are either directly related to them [i.e. the promises of 12.1-3] in the narratives or may be brought into connection with them by the exercise of a little imagination ... the working out of the promises supplies both the main element of tension in the plot of the stories and the primary key to their interpretation.' On 25.21-28, Gerhard von Rad, *Genesis: A Commentary* (OTL; tr. John H. Marks; Philadelphia: Westminster Press, revised edition, 1972), p. 265, sees these verses as 'form[ing] an expository preface to the whole [Jacob story]' and 'acquaint[ing] the reader with those facts which are important for understanding the following stories'. On the Joseph story, Walter Brueggemann writes: 'The power and validity of the dream in 37.5-9 emerge as a main issue. The dream functions in the Joseph narrative as the oracle does for the Jacob materials'; ' ... the dream of chapter 37 governs all that follows' (*Genesis: A Bible Commentary for Teaching and Preaching* [Atlanta: John Knox Press, 1982], pp. 290, 296).

1. *The First Announcement (1.26-28)*

Then God said:

Let us make humankind in our image, after our likeness;
    and let them have dominion over the fish of the sea,
        and over the birds of the air,
        and over the cattle,
        and over all the earth,
        and over every creeping thing that creeps upon the
            earth ...

And God blessed them, and God said to them:

Be fruitful and multiply,
    and fill the earth and subdue it;
    and have dominion over the fish of the sea,
        and over the birds of the air,
        and over every living thing that moves upon the earth.

In this first Announcement of how the plot of Genesis may be expected to develop, three elements come to the fore:

1.   Be fruitful
2.   Subdue the earth
3.   Have dominion over the animals.

Reader-responsively, that is, reading as if for the first time, we are bound to ask, So, do these divine injunctions get fulfilled? Do they form the framework for the plot of Genesis? For— must we not suppose?—if those are the three things that God tells humans to do on the first page of Genesis, the rest of the pages ought to be telling us how the humans carried out the commands, or—at the very least—how they failed to carry out the commands.

Now the one thing that the humans of the early chapters of Genesis seem to be quite successful at is multiplying. By ch. 6 they have begun to multiply on the earth (6.1), and the genealogies of chs. 4, 5, 10, and 11 testify to the quantity of begetting that has been going on. In fact, the only obstacles in the path of the fulfilling of this command are those put there by God himself. For, first, he makes childbearing painful (3.16), then he determines to 'blot out' the whole of the human race with a flood (6.7), and then in ch. 12 he more or less turns a blind eye to the majority of the human race who since the flood have been doing their utmost all over again to be fruitful and multiply (ch. 10), and focuses an almost exclusive attention on one man, as if the whole process has to start afresh from the very beginning.

What this goes to show for the plot of Genesis is that God's commands, even when accompanied by a blessing, do not easily shape themselves into reality, especially because one can never be sure that God himself is not going to sabotage them. The reader can hardly be expected to blame the human race or the patriarchal family for the fact that Genesis ends up with no more than 70 humans who really count for the narrative (46.27), a birthrate of less than one and a half per chapter. It does seem somewhat thoughtless, not to say perverse, to insist on the command to fruitfulness being executed by a family with so many old men and barren women in it.

How does the expectation of subduing the earth fare, then? Adam in Eden no doubt thinks himself master of all he surveys, but the readers know, even if Adam has not yet realized it, that he is to be the 'servant' of the soil, that he has been put in the garden to עבד ('till', 'serve', 'work') it and שמר ('keep') it.[1] So that we wonder who exactly is the master, the poor lonely naked ape himself, or the tropical garden that threatens to run rank if the earth-creature does not solicitously tend it with whatever energy he can muster on his rigorous fruitarian diet. Nothing very masterful happens thereafter, either. East of Eden the earth will yield its produce to hungry humans only if the said humans have sweated over eradicating thorns and thistles from it. And when it comes to the flood story, who is the master then? The humans or the earth they have been supposed to be subduing but which now floods the breath of life from them (6.17)? No doubt the humans bear a fair share of responsibility for what happens to them; but it is hard to deny that the primary reason why the humans do not manage to subdue the earth is because God is constantly making the earth more ferocious and less tameable.

Reading on, then, through the ancestral narratives, we fail to find very much about the humans subduing the earth. They seem to live a fairly precarious and marginal existence, what

1 What danger will it run if it is not 'kept'?, we wonder.

with famines and the problem of finding water and the per-
petual movement in search of more hospitable environments.
The only time nature comes near to being tamed is when
Joseph forestalls the effect of the famine in Egypt by ware-
housing grain for seven years. Was this 'subduing of the earth'
the kind of thing God had in mind in ch. 1, or did he not foresee
the social or economic or ecological consequences of Joseph's
control of the environment? What is to happen, for example, in
the next famine, when the peasants of Egypt have no more
land to sell to the pharaoh (47.19)?

Having dominion over the animals, the third element in the
primal agenda, also proves to have some nasty surprises in
store. Who would have thought, innocently reading Genesis 1,
that on the next page, after its undoubtedly impressive
demonstration of linguistic skills (2.19), the very first animal
in the Bible who does anything very decisively has dominion
over the humans. This does not seem to be what was intended.

In this case, though, God himself is not too happy about the
way the agenda is developing. So first he makes the snake slide
on the ground so that the dust will get into its mouth every
time it tries to start another theological conversation (3.14).
Then, a little later, he decrees that the form the human dominion over animals will take is that humans will cut animals
up into little bits and proceed to masticate them (9.3). This
surprising turn of events is almost as bad for the humans as it
is for the animals, who having only recently been saved from a
watery doom by Noah have reason to think affectionately of
the humans. From the humans' point of view as well, this
provision of protein has its drawback: for who wants to walk
through the world with every living thing being 'in fear and
dread of you', quite apart from the nausea that comes of
knowing that 'every moving thing will be food for you' (9.3).
Slugs?

Thereafter dominion over the animals does not figure very
prominently in Genesis, aside from occasional sacrifices or
feasts. The form it generally takes in the tales about the
Hebrew ancestors is the ownership of a very few species of
animals by the protagonists: mainly sheep, oxen, asses and
camels (e.g. 12.16). And the execution of this element of the
first Announcement is not entirely straightforward. For in

fact having dominion over animals can be something of a lia-
bility when famines hit the land of Canaan and the ancestors
have more than their family's empty stomachs to worry
about. And by the end of Genesis, being encumbered with
flocks of sheep proves to be even worse than a constant source
of anxiety; for on arrival in Egypt the sheep-herding patriarch
Jacob suddenly discovers that 'every shepherd is an abomina-
tion to the Egyptians' (46.34) and finds himself installed in
lonely apartheid in Goshen some way from his favourite son.

What all this means to say is that the initial programme of
Genesis is very inefficiently executed. And it is not all the fault
of the humans, either.

2. *The Second Announcement (12.1-2)*

> Go from your country and your kindred and your father's
>   house
>   to the land that I will show you.
> And I will make of you a great nation,
>   and I will bless you, and make your name great.
> And be a blessing!

With this second Announcement of how the plot of Genesis
may be expected to develop the first Announcement is not set
on one side but, apparently, added to. The reproduction element is turned from a command (1.28) into a prediction (12.2)
and two further expectations are introduced.

The three elements of this Announcement take three different forms. There is the prediction ('I will make of you a
great nation'), the command ('Be a blessing') and a combination of command and prediction ('Go to the land I will show
you'). I will discuss them in this order:

1. Go to the land I will show you
2. Be a blessing
3. I will make of you a great nation.

The first item on this agenda gets off to a shaky start, but
before long seems to be realized firmly enough. The cryptic
command, 'Go to the land I will show you', obviously takes
some decipherment on Abram's part. For though everyone
knows the way to the land of Canaan, what is the way to the

land the Lord will show you? Abram will only know which is
the land when he gets there and the Lord 'shows' him that it *is*
the land. In fact, the first time Abram arrives in the land of
Canaan he walks right through it and out the other side (12.5,
9, 10), presumably because God has not yet said, 'This is the
land!' What God does say when Abram reaches Canaan is,
actually, 'This is the land I am going to give to your descendants' (12.7)—which Abram can only take to mean, 'But not
to you'. Not until the end of ch. 13, after Abram has been deported from Egypt, and is back at Bethel, does God actually
'show' him the land. This time God actually does say, 'to you'
as well as 'to your descendants' (13.15), so Abram at last
knows he has arrived.

The second agendum is, Be a blessing (we note the imperative in 12.2).[1] This blessing that Abram and his descendants
are to spread around is obviously destined for 'all the families
of the earth' (12.3); whether they are to find blessing stream-
ing to them through the Abrahamic family (as the niphal
would suggest in 12.3; 18.18; 28.14) or count themselves fortunate in being associated with the family (as the hithpael would
suggest in 22.18; 26.4) is not perhaps very important to settle;
either way it amounts to much the same thing.

Given this agendum, we are bound to ask, So do the families
of the earth in fact find the Abrahamic family a blessing? We
observe that the first foreigners to be met with in the narrative
are the Canaanites. In two successive sentences we read: 'At
that time the Canaanites were in the land. Then the Lord ...
said to Abram, To your descendants I will give this land' (12.7-
8). This promise can only be described as good news for

---

1 Most scholars evade the force of the imperative with proposals
which usually necessitate revocalization. Cf. various proposals by:
John Skinner, *A Critical and Exegetical Commentary on Genesis*
(ICC; Edinburgh: T. and T. Clark, 2nd edn, 1930), p. 244; E.A.
Speiser, *Genesis* (AB, 1; Garden City, NY: Doubleday, 1983), pp. 85,
86; George W. Coats, *Genesis: With an Introduction to Narrative
Literature* (FOTL, 1; Grand Rapids: Eerdmans, 1983), pp. 107-108;
Theodorus C. Vriezen, 'Bemerkungen zu Genesis 12.1-7', in M.A.
Beek *et al.* (eds.), *Symbolae biblicae et Mesopotamiae F.M.T. de
Liagre Böhl dedicatae* (Leiden: E.J. Brill, 1973), p. 387; Claus
Westermann, *Genesis 12–36: A Commentary* (tr. John J. Scullion;
Minneapolis: Augsburg, 1985), p. 144.

Hebrews but bad news for Canaanites. With blessings like this, who needs curses? Things do not improve a great deal when Abram and Sarai reach Egypt, and encounter their next set of blessable foreigners. The blessing the Egyptians get through the ancestral family are 'great plagues' from the Lord on the Pharaoh and his household. In a cordial exchange of blessings Abram for his part gets, not plagues, but sheep, oxen, he-asses, men-servants, maid-servants, she-asses and camels (12.16), the Egyptian men-servants and maid-servants no doubt reckoning themselves to be greatly blessed being chattels of Abram even though ranking somewhere between he-asses and she-asses.

In the next chapter we find Abram extending his blessing to the four kings who have been reckless enough to include Lot in their booty from Sodom. As if to spread the blessing as widely as possible, Abram pursues the kings as far north as Hobah, beyond Damascus (14.15), routing among others 'Tidal, king of nations' (גוים, 14.9), a neat symbolic gesture of the ancestral family's relation to the wider world. One does not need to be a particularly jaundiced reader of Genesis to observe that the best way to receive this famous Abrahamic blessing is to keep out of the way of the Abrahamic family as far as possible. We have only to think of the fate of the Egyptian Hagar, or of the divine pronouncement to Abimelech king of Gerar, 'You are a dead man because of the woman ... she is a man's wife' (20.3), to be reminded of the effect upon foreigners of the family of Abram and Sarai.

From this perspective the story of Isaac in Gerar takes on fresh meaning. Nothing so drastic happens as when his father had attempted to pass off his wife as his sister, though Isaac has indeed exposed the whole town to the risk of sleeping with Rebekah. 'One of the people might easily have lain with your wife', Abimelech says, none too gallantly, but with understandable trepidation. The worst effect of Isaac's presence in the town is that the perfectly innocuous Philistines have to witness Isaac 'sowing in that land', their land, and 'reaping in the same year a hundredfold' (26.12)—which makes the Philistines realize how fortunate they are to be host to a man so singularly 'blessed of the Lord' (26.12, 29) even though they are not personally having any of the action and the bottom has

fallen out of the wheat market. We are saddened to read that
they 'became envious' (26.14).

The only item on the other pan of the scale is the undoubted
benefit the opportunistic Joseph does to the Egyptians and, for
that matter, to 'all the earth' (41.57) by averting the worst
effects of the famine. Joseph's plan is of course a blessing only
if one would rather be a live slave than a dead peasant. The
narrative makes no bones about it, though the Masoretic text
is understandably squeamish: the narrative is no doubt meant
to say that Joseph 'made slaves of them from one end of Egypt
to the other' (47.21) (העביד אתו לעבדים). It is the Samaritan text
that preserves the unpleasant truth which the Masoretes
could only attempt to palliate when they chose as their text
העביר אתו לערים, 'removed them to the cities'—itself a less than
brilliant solution to the problems of a food shortage.

The third element of the Announcement, 'I will make of
you a great nation', does not lead to total disappointment, but
neither can there be said to be a truly adequate success in
fulfilling it. There should be, since the execution of this element, is very largely if not entirely up to God. There would no
doubt be rather more success if the Lord did not persist in
making things so difficult for himself, engineering matriar-
chal barrennesses, famines, and murderous feuds between
brothers.

The only progress that has been made by the end of Genesis
towards establishing a great nation is that there are seventy
persons of the house of Jacob in 46.26, admittedly not including
Jacob's sons' wives, or, presumably, Jacob's sons' wives' maid-
servants. Considering the difficulties, we could perhaps allow
that a promising start has been made. The fact that they are
now all in the wrong country hardly seems to matter.

What then can we say happens to the Abrahamic
Announcement of ch. 12 by the end of Genesis? The first element ('Go to the land I will show you') has, near enough, been
fulfilled, both the going and the showing. The fact that the
ancestral family ends up out of the land is not an insurmount-
able problem, because they are very conscious that they are
headed back toward the land in the near future, Joseph
solemnly promising his older brothers as he dies at the
advanced age of 110 that they will return to Canaan, carrying

Joseph's bones (50.25). No record is given of how his centenarian brothers responded to this parting shot by Joseph who is evidently still intent on wreaking his revenge on them for getting him to Egypt in the first place. Fortunately, from their point of view, Joseph was wrong by a factor of 430 years, according to Exod. 12.40, and this little announcement of the future on Joseph's part is not translated into reality in just the way it might have been expected to be.

The second element, 'Be a blessing', is an almost complete disaster, the one foreigner to benefit unambiguously from the patriarchal family's existence being the pharaoh who now rules a nation of slaves. It comes as a disappointment to readers anxious for the fulfilment of the announcements of plot to learn, when they get into Exodus 1, that there has arisen a pharaoh who does not know Joseph. For this implies that the one blessing the Hebrew ancestors ever did for any of the 'families of the earth' is now completely forgotten.

The third element, 'I will make of you a great nation', is at least on the road to execution by the time Genesis ends. It is a little disconcerting, all the same, to find, when the family does re-appear in Canaan in ch. 50 for the burial of Jacob in a proleptic mini-exodus, that 'all the servants of Pharaoh ... and all the elders of the land of Egypt' accompany them (50.7), and the gawping Canaanites remark on what an impression these 'Egyptians' are making (50.11). This cannot be an entirely satisfactory episode for a family expecting to become a 'great nation' in its own right.

3. *The Third Announcement (25.23; 27.27-29, 39-40)*

Two peoples, born of you, shall be divided;
   the one shall be stronger than the other,
   the elder shall serve the younger (25.23).

May God give you [Jacob] of the dew of heaven,
   and of the fatness of the earth
   and plenty of grain and wine.
Let peoples serve you,
   and nations bow down to you.
Be lord over your brothers,
   and may your mother's sons bow down to you (27.28-29).

> Behold, away from the fatness of the earth shall your
>   dwelling be [Esau]
>   and away from the dew of heaven on high.
> By your sword you shall live,
>   and you shall serve your brother (27.39-40).

The Announcement relating to Jacob and Esau is contained in three passages. The first is the birth oracle (25.23) which predicts that the two twins will be divided from one another and the elder son will serve the younger. The second and third are Isaac's blessings on the two sons. A large number of motifs are deployed in these blessings; for convenience' sake we may group the principal motifs under three headings:

1. service
2. fertility
3. division.

The first element, service, is the idea that Esau should serve Jacob, the verb עבד occurring in each of the three passages to indicate this. We are therefore expecting the narrative to tell us of this serving. The fact is, however, that apart from passages that promise or desire that Esau should serve Jacob, all the 'serving' that gets done in the Jacob story is by Jacob. The seventeen occurrences of עָבַד, עֶבֶד or עֲבֹדָה are in reference to Jacob's serving, none to Esau's.[1] Jacob serves his uncle Laban (29.15), not only for money but even for his wives, even though they are of the same family (29.20, 30). He even gets himself 'hired out' as a serving man to satisfy Leah's sexual appetites (30.16). Much more significant, though, is the way he projects himself, in his meeting with Esau. 'When my brother Esau meets you', he says to his retainers, 'you shall say, These belong to your servant Jacob' (32.17, 18). No matter that this is Jacob at his most obsequious; his words in fact amount to an inversion of the blessing he had earlier risked so much to gain. And whereas in 27.29 Isaac had hoped that nations would bow down (השׁתחוה) to Jacob, the only bowing down in the whole Jacob cycle is done by Jacob and his family, in a comic surfeit of prostration, himself seven times, then the secondary wives

---

1 עֶבֶד: 32.4, 11, 19, 20; 33.14; עָבַד: 29.15, 18, 20, 25, 27, 30; 30.26 (2x), 29; 31.6; עֲבֹדָה: 29.27; 30.26.

and their children, then Leah and her children, then Joseph and Rachel (33.3, 6-7). Jacob serves everyone; no one serves Jacob. So much for the blessing.

The second element in what is wished for Jacob is fertility— with corresponding infertility for Esau (27.28, 39). Now it is true that this is realized for him: he becomes 'exceedingly rich, with large flocks, maidservants and manservants, and camels and asses' (30.43, the servants ranking this time after the flocks and before the camels). There is the slight difficulty that his favourite wife is barren, but otherwise fertility is the rule of the house. What is surprising about the outworking of the fertility wishes is that Esau, who by all expectation ought to be getting a negative blessing, is also prospering quite satisfactorily. Being without the birthright and the first son's blessing has not obviously done him much harm, not if he can bring to the meeting with Jacob a band of 400 men (32.6; 33.1) which are obviously so many more than Jacob's company that Jacob is frightened out of his wits (32.7). And when Jacob gingerly invites Esau to accept his 'present', calling it with unimaginable insensitivity his 'blessing' (ברכה), Esau can say with equal truth and equanimity, 'I have enough, my brother; keep what you have for yourself' (33.9). The brother with the blessing is more needy than the one without.

The third element is division, the implication of the birth oracle being that the division between the brothers will signify hostility and dissension. This is indeed what happens throughout the greater part of the narrative. But the surprise the story has in store for us is that after what seems like a lifetime of division, including murderous plans by Esau (27.41) and physical separation, the narrative moves towards an effectual reconciliation. Esau holds nothing against Jacob any longer, but runs to meet him, falls on his neck and kisses him, and they both weep (33.4). They separate physically again but not emotionally. The official explanation given by the narrator in 36.6-8 for why the brothers do not live together is that they simply do not have enough room for their cattle, Esau no less wealthy than Jacob. The scene reminds us of the separation of Abram and Lot, a separation that was equally amicable and equally constructive for the growth of the ancestral family. The primal birth oracle is not exactly overturned, because it was somewhat Delphic in its wording anyway. But, following on the uterine conflict of the twins, it led us to imagine the worst for the relationship of the brothers. In that respect we were not deceived—not, that is, till the close of the story where a quite different nuance was laid upon the term 'divide', and we discovered that it meant mere physical separation without any emotional dissension.

In sum, the Announcements that preface the Jacob story are on the whole misleading about the course that the action of the narrative will take.[1]

4. *The Fourth Announcement (37.5-10)*

Now Joseph had a dream...
Hear this dream, which I have dreamed:
behold, we were binding sheaves in the field,
    and lo, my sheaf arose and stood upright;
and behold your sheaves gathered around it,
    and bowed down to my sheaf... (37.5-7).

Then he dreamed another dream ...
Behold, I have dreamed another dream;
and behold, the sun, the moon, and the eleven stars were
    bowing down to me (37.9).

The fourth Announcement of Genesis takes the form of two dreams of Joseph purporting to foretell the future. They predict, according to the interpretations of them proffered in vv. 8 and 10, that:

1. Joseph's brothers will bow down to him
2. The brothers, and the father and mother, will bow down to him.

What happens to this Announcement, in brief, is that the first element comes true, and the second does not. The brothers bow down before him four times in Egypt (42.6; 43.26, 28; 44.14). But his father never does. In fact it is Joseph who bows

---

1 This view differs from that of most commentators; e.g. Brueggemann, *Genesis*, p. 208: 'Without a very explicit statement, the narrative [33.1-17] affirms that the initial oracle of 25.23 has come to fruition'.

before Jacob (48.12).[1] And his mother of course cannot. For Rachel has already died in 35.16-19 in childbirth with Benjamin, as Jacob will remind us in 48.7. Benjamin is certainly alive in ch. 37 because there are eleven stars bowing down to him. But his mother is dead. So Jacob knows that Joseph's dream cannot be fulfilled. Well, not exactly. But he is

---

1 Commentators regularly fail to see this point; cf., for example, von Rad, *Genesis*, pp. 352, 383. Robert Alter, commenting on 42.6 in 'Joseph and His Brothers', *Commentary* (November, 1980), pp. 59-69 (62) (= *The Art of Biblical Narrative* [London: George Allen and Unwin, 1981], p. 163), states, 'Joseph's two dreams are here literally fulfilled'. Yet, to reach this conclusion he is compelled to interpret the imagery of the sun, moon and stars as foreshadowing Joseph's role as Egyptian vizier—which is certainly not how Jacob understands the dream! (cf. further Alter, *The Art of Biblical Narrative*, p. 169). Eric I. Lowenthal, in *Commentary* (February, 1981), pp. 17-18 (18), responding to Alter, rightly takes him to task by pointing out that, whereas the dream spoke of eleven stars, only ten brothers bow down in 42.6. Unfortunately, he does not develop this insight. Gibson, *Genesis*, vol. 2, p. 273, writes: 'We are left in no doubt that this was a fulfilment, partial maybe but real, of the dreams in chapter 37'. It would be closer to the truth to say that the first dream is eventually fulfilled (with Benjamin's bowing down in 43.26), but that only one of the three elements of the second dream (obeisance of the eleven brothers) has been fulfilled. Donald A. Seybold, 'Paradox and Symmetry in the Joseph Narrative', in Kenneth R.R. Gros Louis, with James S. Ackerman and Thayer S. Warshaw (eds.), *Literary Interpretations of Biblical Narratives* (Nashville: Abingdon Press, 1974), p. 69, points out that in 42.6 'the second dream remains unfulfilled,' but he is very vague on any actual fulfilment of it (cf. p. 72). Wolfgang Richter, 'Traum und Traumdeutung im AT: Ihre Form und Verwendung', *Biblische Zeitschrift* 7 (1963), pp. 202-20 (208), believes that the fulfilment of the first dream (42.6ff.) prepares the way for the fulfilment of the second, which is achieved, though not literally (*wörtlich*), in ch. 47. He too remains vague on how the second dream works out. We may ask, If it is not fulfilled literally, how can it be said to have been fulfilled at all, when all other dreams in the Joseph story are fulfilled literally? Apparently the only scholar to read 48.12 in the light of 37.5-11 is Gibson, *Genesis*, vol. 2, pp. 230-31, who comments on Joseph's prostration before Jacob: 'It is not so commonly pointed out however, that the second dream is not fulfilled in the epic ... Joseph's dream of the sun and moon and stars must have been a false one, suggested by his own arrogance and ambition, and not at all by God's prompting.'

pious, or superstitious, enough to wonder whether there may not be some truth in it even so. So he keeps his options open, or as the Hebrew has it, 'kept the matter' (שמר את הדבר). But he makes not the slightest effort to fulfil his part in bringing it to pass.

Conclusion

Joseph's dreams may be taken as a paradigm for how Announcements function in Genesis. Because they have been spoken by someone with authority, like God or a patriarch or a dreamer, the reader must reckon with the possibility that they may be executed. But only the possibility. Reality as it develops in Genesis has a rather unpredictable connection with the Announcements disclosing how it is supposed to develop.

If we are trying to guess the likelihood of an announcement becoming reality, we cannot proceed by distinguishing between what God says and what humans say, as though divine words were bound to be more reliable predictors of coming events.[1] Nor do we have any more success if we discriminate between what is commanded, what is promised, and what is wished for. Nor is it always very clear whether a particular thing announced has actually come about or not.

Perhaps there is a basic flaw in the approach I have adopted. Was I right in supposing that what is announced in Genesis should be expected to be fulfilled in Genesis? It seemed to be a reasonable assumption, but let us allow that it might be more apt to regard Genesis as simply the first volume in a larger sequence of narrative works *à la recherche du temps perdu*, Genesis–2 Kings. It is indeed incontrovertible that the narrative begun by Genesis does not really come to a pause—as a narrative—until the end of 2 Kings; but there it does come

---

1 This is in opposition to the view of Peter D. Miscall, 'The Jacob and Joseph Stories as Analogies', *JSOT* 6 (1978), pp. 28-40 (32), who believes that one must distinguish in biblical narrative between divine and human words in the following way: with divine words (e.g. prophecy, oracle), 'it is a question not of whether it will be fulfilled but of how it will be fulfilled', whereas with human words (e.g. blessing, prediction), 'it is a matter of whether it will be fulfilled, and not just of how'.

to a full stop, and any extension of the narrative can only be possible by telling the story all over again from the beginning, starting again with Adam, Seth, Enosh (1 Chr. 1.1).

Genesis, that is to say, starts a narrative chain that concludes with 2 Kings 25. So, in order to answer our initial question more comprehensively, perhaps we need to ask, What happens to the Announcements by the point the narrative has reached at the end of 2 Kings? Perhaps 'what happens in Genesis' can only be stated once we have read to the end of the story as a totality. So, what *has* happened?

The first set of announcements, in Genesis 1, presents an agenda that is not explicitly said to have been carried out, but neither has it failed. Even though by the end of 2 Kings the Jewish people is decimated, the human race at large has been adequately prolific and there is at least no shortage of Chaldaeans and Egyptians. The earth has been filled and subdued: there are no more famines, in the land or out of it, that may be laid to the account of the earth; only humans create starvation (2 Kgs 25.2-3). Wild animals are no threat to the stability of states, and human dominion over animals as beasts of burden and as food is too much taken for granted to be remarked upon. The animal kingdom has indeed experienced a major reprieve through the destruction of the Jerusalem temple, but no one represents that as any derogation of human power over the animals.

But with the second set of Announcements things are quite different. If Genesis 12 announces that the Abrahamic family is to become a great nation, 2 Kings tells us that in the end this did not happen. The 10,000 significant members of the nation still surviving at the end of the narrative sequence (2 Kgs 24.14) are carried into Babylon, where they may be presumed to lose the status of a nation. And the insignificant members go, 'all' of them (25.26), to Egypt, and equally to oblivion. Whatever happened to the promise between Genesis and 2 Kings, and whatever nationhood the Abrahamic family acquired in the bygoing, has been undermined by the end of 2 Kings.

And if Genesis announces that Abraham and his descendants will be given a land, 2 Kings reports that in the end the family of Abraham ended up precisely in Babylonia and Egypt, for all the world as if they had never left Ur or as if Abram,

Sarai and Lot had never escaped from Genesis 12. In case we needed the point spelled out, 2 Kgs 25.21 observes, amazingly laconically: 'So Judah was taken into exile out of its land'. It does not need to say, The land promised by Yahweh. We know that.

And then if Genesis announces divine blessing for the Abrahamic family, and a covenanted divine-human relationship, 2 Kings reports: 'It came to the point in Jerusalem and Judah that he cast them out of his presence'. And as for the intended blessing to the nations, we wonder whether the arrival of 7000 mercenaries and 1000 carpenters and smiths in Babylon, along with their numerous dependants and various nonentities (2 Kgs 24.16; 25.11) constitutes a blessing commensurate with the effort expended in getting all the way from Genesis to 2 Kings.

In short, Israel's Primary History, the narrative sequence of Genesis–2 Kings, is a narrative of (in the end) unmitigated disaster, and Genesis' story of the failure to meet the programme set forth by its Announcements is no contrast to the Primary History as a whole, but rather presages the direction in which the larger story is headed. In fact, Genesis distracts us, to a certain extent, from recognizing what the future course of events in the Primary History will inevitably be by suggesting that to some degree the Announcements are coming true. For, according to the narrative of Genesis to 2 Kings, despite appearances, they do not.[1]

---

1 For further elaboration of this reading of the Primary History, see Chapter 4 below.

Chapter 3

THE ANCESTOR IN DANGER:
BUT NOT THE SAME DANGER*

The study of the stories commonly known as the 'ancestress in danger' narratives, in Genesis 12, 20, and 26, has in the past been rendered systematically unsatisfactory by two *idées fixes*.

The first is a minor one, which can soon be neutralized. It is that these stories are essentially tales of the *ancestress*, or perhaps rather that what makes them interesting as tales is the danger confronting the ancestress. There is indeed quite a lot of danger about in these narratives of adventures in foreign parts, so one could hardly claim that there is no danger at all to the ancestress. But what the texts of these tales makes plain is that the person who *feels* threatened is not the matriarch at all but always the patriarch. So in 12.12 Abram is sure that when the Egyptians see Sarai they will say, 'This is his wife'; 'then they will kill me', he says, 'but they will let you live.' There are no doubt fates worse than death, but none that Abram can imagine, not even for Sarai, and certainly not for himself.

In ch. 20 too, Abraham openly says that he thought there would be no fear of God in Gerar, and that its inhabitants would kill him because of Sarah (20.11)—which not only proves to be as wrong as it is possible to be, but also causes us to reflect on what 'fear of God' Abraham personally entertains when he lies about Sarah's blood relationship to him and asks for many other like offences to be taken into consideration in mitigation of the present one (20.12-13). In ch. 26 as well, Isaac no less than Abraham justifies the same deception on the

* An earlier version of this Chapter was read as a paper to the Biblical Criticism and Literary Criticism Section of the Society of Biblical Literature at its Annual Meeting in Atlanta, November 25, 1986.

ground of his fear: 'he feared to say, "My wife", thinking "lest
the men of the place should kill me for the sake of Rebekah";
because she was fair to look upon' (26.7). And to Abimelech's
face he candidly admits his fear with the words, 'Because I
thought, Lest I die because of her'. Laying down one's life for
one's wife is evidently no ideal in this patriarchal society.

There may of course be a certain scholarly gallantry in play
in making out that in these stories it is the *ancestress* that is
endangered. Patriarchs can surely look after themselves (and
do, if these tales are anything to go by), but matriarchs are
vulnerable in a patriarchal world. What such a gallantry disguises is that the danger is all in the patriarch's mind to begin
with, and, in addition, that the actual danger in the narratives
is mainly of the patriarch's making. So calling these stories
'The Ancestor in Danger' seems to be a more appropriate
focus, since that is the complication that sets each of these stories in motion. We might, nevertheless, wonder whether in
fact the biggest danger is to either the ancestress or the
ancestor, and not rather to some other element in the story,
like the plot or else the achievement of what is supposed to be
happening in Genesis. Whether that is indeed the case will
have to transpire later.

The more important idea about these stories that is long over-
due for re-evaluation is the conviction that these three narratives are 'really' one narrative, a 'thrice-told tale' in David
Petersen's phrase.[1] It may well of course be true, and I indeed
think it very probable, that what was once one tale now lies
before us in three versions. But where that inference about the
prehistory of Genesis is utterly unsatisfactory is that it cannot
explain why the tale is told three times in Genesis, nor what
the point of each of the tellings, at the specific places where
they are located, can be.[2]

1 David L. Petersen, 'A Thrice-Told Tale: Genre, Theme and Motif in
   Genesis 12, 20 and 26', *Biblical Research* 18 (1973), pp. 30-43.
2 Robert Polzin's paper, '"The Ancestress in Danger" in Danger'
   (*Semeia* 3 [1975] 81-98), at first sight may seem to promise to carry
   out a similar project to the present one. His protest against the exclusively diachronic analyses of these stories would have been a
   suitable preface for a contextual reading of them; one can note his

My idea is simply to read each tale strictly in the light of the Genesis story so far, reader-responsively refusing to let my knowledge of what is going to happen in the story hereafter influence my reading of the tale before my eyes—until I choose to, that is, and very deliberately noting what differences hindsight makes to the reading and what new levels of meaning it adds to a tale that already has its own significance at this particular juncture within the developing story.

1. *The First Story (Genesis 12.10-20)*

With the first of the 'danger' stories (Gen 12.10-20), there are just three pieces of information from the foregoing narrative that are crucial for understanding the tale *in context*. The first is that Yahweh has promised Abram that he will make from him a great nation, which can only mean that Abram will have many descendants. The second is that Abram's wife Sarai is barren (11.30). The third is that Abram was accompanied by Lot, the son of his dead younger brother (11.27-28; 12.4-5).

Now these three items amount to a plot. That is to say: the man, who has been promised children, but who cannot have children by his wife, has, however, a nephew. The nephew, who lacks a father, can become the son of the man who lacks children.

If we review these plot elements from the point of view of Abram we understand how the character Abram behaves. When he hears the divine promise that he will be made into a great nation, he cannot believe that Sarai will have anything to do with the fulfilment of that promise. Her barrenness is a datum of both their lives. Yahweh has not said that the line of Abram's descendants will be through his own literal son, so how else can Abram imagine the promise being realized than through the son of his dead brother? From Abram's point of

bewailing of the current 'lack of concern for how [the] stories fit into their present literary context ... the larger story-line of the present patriarchal narratives' (p. 82). In fact, however, his reading also is almost wholly concerned with the relationships between the three narratives, and not with their settings in the larger narrative of Genesis.

view, which is equally the perspective of the reader of the 'story so far', Lot is the only possible candidate for the channel of fulfilment of the promise.

This understanding makes quite a difference to how the wife-sister tale of this chapter is to be read. In this perspective Sarai is disposable, expendable; she has nothing to contribute to the realization of the promise. However attached to her Abram may be, nothing hangs upon her continued survival. Abram and Lot are the ones who must be preserved in Egypt, at all cost. In a way, of course, if Lot already is the son, nothing hangs upon Abram's survival either, but if Abram is to 'become' a great nation, perhaps he needs to be still alive in order to see it happen. And in any case, we do not know how old this son/nephew Lot is, or whether he may be still in need of Abram's protection (as he certainly will be in ch. 14, even when he is a grown man).

The danger in this story is, on this reading, a danger to Abram's life, and, more seriously, a danger to the fulfilment of the prediction if Abram does *not* ensure that he and Lot survive the Egyptian experience. There is a danger to the plot and to what the announcements of it have promised the readers of the book.

Furthermore, this perspective is determinative for a preliminary ethical judgment on Abram. Whatever may be said of the means he chooses for the preservation of the promise, and whatever may be said about the very idea of thinking it is necessary to do anything at all for the success of a divine promise, the story makes it plain what Abram's motivation is, and invites us to return a judgment in accordance with that. We might phrase it somewhat differently from Calvin, but find it difficult not to echo his sentiments, so long, that is, that we read this tale in the light of the 'story so far':

> Abram had far higher ends in view... Undoubtedly, he would have chosen to die a hundred times, rather than thus to ruin the character of his wife, and to be deprived of the society of her whom alone he loved. But while he reflected that the hope of salvation was centred in himself, ... that unless he lived, the benediction promised to him, and to his seed, was vain; he did not estimate his own life according to the private affection of the flesh; but inasmuch as he did not wish the

effect of the divine vocation to perish through his death, he
was so affected with concern for the preservation of his own
life, that he overlooked every thing besides. So far, then, he
deserves praise ...[1]

That little phrase, 'so far, then', says a great deal about how
wider considerations will impinge on the issue, but for the
moment we are invited by the story to adopt Abram's standpoint.

Now, not only is Abram's deception explained by the present
reading, but also some details of the narrative become intelli-
gible for the first time. Why, first, should it be said when
Abram has been told by Yahweh to 'go' (using the singular)
from his country (12.1), leaving behind his 'kindred' and his
'father's house', not only that 'Abram went, as Yahweh had
told him' but also that 'Lot also went with him' (12.4)?
Perhaps we might reply, Because Lot is later to figure in the
story of Abraham in Canaan, and we had better be told explicitly that he actually left Haran. That is not of course to
explain the notation by the 'story so far', and while we can
accept that narrative foreshadowings are not always explica-
ble by the preceding action, the second notation makes us
wonder whether we are dealing simply with foreshadowing
and not with hints that are significant for the *present* narrative. For, secondly, in the immediately following verse it is said
that 'Abram took Sarai his wife, and Lot his brother's son ...
and they set forth to go to the land of Canaan' (12.5). In the
third place, we note the remark at the end of the Egyptian
episode: 'And Abram went up from Egypt, he and his wife and
all that was his, and Lot with him' (13.1). The slight syntactic
awkwardness of the reference to Lot foregrounds his presence. It would have been enough if at 13.5 Lot should have
been mentioned for the first time after our original introduction to him: 'And also Lot, who went with Abram, had flocks
and herds and tents'. Lot, we infer, has an implicit significance
for the story of ch. 12, just as he has an explicit significance for
the story of ch. 13.

This is now the moment for us to read the narrative again,

1 John Calvin, *A Commentary on Genesis* (r.p. London: Banner of
Truth Trust, 1965), p. 359.

this time with the hindsight that comes of knowing how the Abraham story as a whole will develop. This time we know that, since Sarah is to be the mother of the one legitimate channel of fulfilment for the promise, there is an important danger to her and therewith to the promise itself. An irony arises: Far from being the expendable member of the trio, as Abram thinks, she is essential, as we second-time readers know. And the narrative interest consists very largely in the tension between the first reading and all subsequent readings.

2. *The Second Story (Genesis 20)*

When we turn to the second of the 'ancestor in danger' stories (ch. 20), we must once again enquire about the context in which it is set. It is a much more complex context, from which we can separate out three strands of plot, concerning, respectively, Lot, Ishmael and Isaac.

a. *Lot*

The Lot strand has run right through the intervening narrative, from the beginning of ch. 13 right up to the last verse of the previous chapter (19.37-38). In ch. 13 we saw how Lot took possession (so to speak) of part of the promised land on behalf of the Abrahamic family, and in the process entrenched himself yet further in its destiny. Far from the more usual reading of the chapter as a wistful parting of the ways between Abram and Lot, the narrative to my mind plainly depicts Lot settling in the most desirable part of the promised land, which Yahweh has at this very moment just 'shown' to Abram as the land he intends to be held by Abram 'and [his] descendants' (13.15). Lot is Abram's descendant, and at this point his only descendant; his settling in the valley of the Jordan, unquestionably a part of the 'land', is proof of that. In ch. 14, Abram is rescuing Lot from the confederate kings, not from a mere humanitarian impulse or out of a kinsman's sense of duty, but because Lot's death or absence from the land will mean the removal of Abram's only descendant.

The Lot thread continues. In ch. 15 we find Abram bewailing the fact that he has no true son of his own to inherit the gifts that Yahweh is promising him (the claimed reference to a slave named Eliezer of Damascus [cf. 15.2-3] is highly dubious, as the commentators say, and the person in question, 'a son of my house' and not 'my own seed', sounds very much like the only other male of the family we have met, namely Lot). This does not mean that Abram has been recently developing an urge to have a son of his very own and is now attempting to manipulate Yahweh into precisely that promise that Yahweh is about to deliver; nor that Abram is disenchanted with Lot; nor that Lot is no longer his descendant. These are the wistful words of an old man who realizes he is about to 'pass on' (הלך) without achieving what every red-blooded Israelite male is supposed to achieve.

Lot is next in view in ch. 18, where Abraham's bargaining over Sodom is self-evidently a story of the patriarch's concern for his kinsman or perhaps for someone who is rather more than merely a kinsman. The point of all this attention to Lot becomes apparent to the first-time reader with ch. 19, however. There we find the promise of progeny to Abraham beginning to take effect, for Lot becomes the father of Moab and Ammon—which means, as the narrator goes out of his way to inform us (19.37-38), that there will be 'one day' (the narrator's 'to this day') whole nations of Moabites and Ammonites who are descendants of Abraham. Even second-time readers, who know of a future twist in the plot, will have no reason to revise their view of Lot as a member of the Abrahamic family, and will see in this episode nothing other than a realization of the promise, triply noted, that Abraham will become the father of a '*multitude* of nations' (17.4-6), not just of a single 'nation'.

b. *Ishmael*
A second strand of the plot has been developing around Ishmael. If we have been blind to the role of Lot, and have been looking elsewhere for a solution to the problem, Who is going to be the channel of fulfilment of the divine promise?, the Ishmael story strikes us at first as curious. For the ostensible reason why Ishmael becomes a twinkle in Abram's eye is not as a potential fulfilment of the promise, but as an answer to Sarai's desire for a child: 'perhaps I shall obtain children by [Hagar]', she says (16.2). In the event, of course, any son of

Sarai's, even by a surrogate mother, is a son of Abram's, and the narrative that began by being professedly concerned with a son for Sarai is at the end interested in Abram rather than Sarai. So it concludes: 'And Hagar bore Abram a son; and Abram called the name of his son, whom Hagar bore, Ishmael' (16.15), Sarai having dropped out of consideration altogether. But what is it about this son that Abram is interested in? Even though in 15.4 Yahweh has promised that Abram's heir will be one who 'comes forth from [his] loins', we doubt that Abram believes it. What Abram 'believes' in this episode is God's second speech, 'So shall your descendants be' (15.5), not his first speech, 'Your own son shall be your heir' (15.4)—to which Abram has made no response and on which the narrator has made no comment. There is nothing at this juncture to convince us that Abram is investing his hopes of succession in Ishmael. If anything, we rather feel throughout chs. 15 and 16 that he cannot be viewing Ishmael as the heir of the promise if he so readily accedes to Sarai's treatment of Hagar, with its predictable outcome of the pregnant Hagar decamping from the Abrahamic household. It is something of a new twist to the plot when in the subsequent chapter Yahweh announces that Abraham will become the father of a multitude of nations (17.4-6)—which must sound to Abraham like the nations that Lot and now also Ishmael will give rise to. This is the point at which Abraham begins to take Ishmael seriously, expressing his emotional commitment to him in his plea for his continued life (17.18), and following up on the promise of Isaac by circumcising Ishmael (17.23-27)! By the end of ch. 17, with Lot temporarily absent from the main action of the plot, Abraham has come to accept Ishmael as the fulfilment of the promise, at the very moment that a third son, who will supplant Ishmael, is being promised. When Abraham at the beginning of ch. 22 hears the divine command to sacrifice Isaac, he will be thinking that he has seen this movie before.

c. *Isaac*

In the third strand of the plot of Genesis between chs. 12 and 20, the future child, named in advance as Isaac (17.19), is promised as a child of Abraham and Sarah. Abraham's response, which has him prostrate with laughter, shows us clearly enough where his thoughts have been leading. His outburst, 'O that Ishmael might live in thy sight!' (17.18), means that he does not believe in this future son and is perfectly content with the one he now has. From Abraham's point of view there is no particular value in this future son. No son can be more his own son than Lot is already, especially now that he now represents the Abrahamic family abroad, so to speak, in the cities of the plain; no son can be more Abraham's own son than Ishmael is already, a son of his own loins and circumcised as sign of his inheritance of the Abrahamic promises.

Even Yahweh in his numerous speeches is unable to make any satisfactory distinction between the significance of the son that is and that of the son yet to be born. For, according to Yahweh, Hagar's descendants (through Ishmael, of course) will be so greatly multiplied that they cannot be numbered for multitude (16.10; 17.20), and the divine covenant is established with Ishmael and his offspring no differently than with all the Abrahamic descendants—that is, the covenant to be God to them and to give them land, which is to say, the covenant of which circumcision is the sign (17.7, 9; cf. 22-27). All the same, the fact is that the divine promise is of a child for Abraham and Sarah, to be born, from the perspective of ch. 17, at 'this time next year' (17.21), or, from the perspective of ch. 18, 'in the spring of the year' (18.10), 'at the season [already mentioned], viz. the spring of the year' (18.14; the Hebrew is not so certain).

d. *The visit to Gerar*

At this very moment, when Lot has just written himself strongly back into the saga, and when Ishmael has come of age (17.25) and Abraham is praying for his preservation (17.18), but a third son, Isaac, has been promised (17.19)—at this very juncture, we must notice, Abraham passes off Sarah as his sister. There is one further item of information, implicit indeed in the arithmetic of the narrative, but impressively meaningful: at the time of the visit to Gerar, Sarah is pregnant.[1] For if there were twelve months to run from 17.21 to

1 One of the few scholars to make this observation is Peter D. Miscall, *The Workings of Old Testament Narrative* (Philadelphia: Fortress

the birth of Isaac, and nine months from 18.10 to the birth of
Isaac, and Isaac is to be born immediately the wife-sister narrative concludes—which is to say: promptly and explicitly 'at
the season of which Yahweh had spoken' (21.2)—Sarah has to
be pregnant during the dangerous incident of ch. 20.

What this must mean, in the first place, is that at the beginning of ch. 20 Abraham still does not believe in Yahweh's
promise of Isaac. If he did, he would know that the child is in
danger if Sarah is in danger. He might even realize that to
whatever extent Sarai might have been dispensable in ch. 12,
she is indispensable here. If anyone is expendable now, it is
Abraham. And what is Abraham doing in Gerar anyway? He
does not have the justification of a famine, as he had in ch. 12.
His journey to Gerar is unmotivated. He has been settled at
Mamre since as long ago as 13.18, which means for the last
fourteen years (cf. 16.16 with 17.17).[1] The narrative feigns
that Abraham is still on the move in search of a homeland,
with its transparent itinerary style: 'from there Abraham
journeyed toward the territory of the Negeb ... and he so-
journed in Gerar' (20.1). But it does not deceive us; it is plain
enough that this is no purposeful journey but an aimless up-
rooting of the family, an almost feckless heading into trouble.

The narrative demands from us an ethical judgment on
Abraham here, not primarily for the lie and the deception,
though we are pretty sure now that Sarah is *not* his half-sis-
ter, hearing his claim embedded among those other examples
of obfuscation, the patriarch protesting too much to convince
us of anything (20.11-13). Abraham earns the reader's disap-
proval rather for his refusal to accept the divine prediction or
to imagine what the consequences of the move to Gerar might
be if perchance the divine word could be coming true and

Press, 1983), p. 32.

1 It is amusing, incidentally, to watch the commentators pretending
   they do not know where Abraham last was; cf. Gerhard von Rad,
   Genesis (OTL; London: SCM Press, 1961), p. 221; Claus Westermann, *Genesis 12–36. A Commentary* (tr. John J. Scullion; Minneapolis: Augsburg, 1985), p. 320. E.A. Speiser, *Genesis* (AB, 1;
   Garden City, NY: Doubleday, 1964), p. 148, in a fit of false naivety
   thinks that 'from there' could only refer in the present context to
   Lot's cave!

Sarah could, against all the odds, be pregnant after all. We ourselves as readers may at this moment still be tempted to keep our options open and our fingers crossed, not yet knowing for sure how the prediction of Isaac may in reality be fulfilled, if at all.

The danger, from the point of view of the 'story so far', is a danger to Abraham, but not the danger he thinks. He fears he is in a godless town, where he may well be killed because of his wife (20.11); in fact it is a godfearing place, ruled by a moralistic king (20.9) who has conversations with God in dreams (20.3-7). The real danger is the danger to the promise which Abraham has received. For we readers suspect, even if Abraham will not believe it, and even if Yahweh himself has not said unequivocally that the only way the promise is going to be fulfilled is by this child of pregnant Sarah's, that the promise somehow hangs upon Isaac.

Even in the outturn, it must be said, we are to be left in some doubt about just what Isaac will be that Ishmael will not be. Ishmael, as well as Isaac, is to be made into a nation (21.13), in addition to being multiplied so greatly as to outdo the sand of the sea (16.10) and being circumcised and in covenant with Yahweh (17.7, 23). The one thing that will be said of Isaac that is not said of Ishmael is that 'in Isaac shall your descendants be called' (21.12), a sentence 'not readily comprehensible', as Westermann[1] remarks. Anyway, this is not a question in the 'story so far'.

It is enough for our present purpose to affirm that in this story of 'the ancestor in danger', unlike the story of ch. 12, the real danger to the ancestor is not the one he thinks. And the danger he is actually in is rather more important for the plot than the danger to the ancestress, who, admittedly, no doubt risks her neck if she is found in the harem of Abimelech to be pregnant with another man's child.

With the hindsight of how the total narrative will develop, what we find in addition to what the 'story so far' tells us is that Isaac will indeed be the only descendant of Abraham who really matters for the plot of Genesis, despite the red herrings of the text of the last seven chapters. And the safe birth of the

1 Westermann, *Genesis 12–36,* p. 340.

promised son is only the beginning of troubles for the promise
on its way to fulfilment; it will have to survive more than mere
threats and possibilities of failure before it is established with
any kind of reasonable certitude. But above all, the extra element that the 'story hereafter' superimposes upon our reading of ch. 20 in the light of the 'story so far' is that Abraham
and Sarah only realize after they have been deported from
Gerar that Sarah had been pregnant all the time—which
means that they have had a very near brush with disaster. In
ch. 20 the danger was very much more complex than
Abraham imagined or than the narrator makes explicit.

3. *The Third Story (Genesis 26)*

Now in the case of the third of our stories, the narrative context is different again. By this stage, the 'story so far' includes
not only the sweep of the patriarchal history, but also the two
previous wife-sister stories, to which the narrative now insists
that we make connections. Thus not only is ch. 26 *like* ch. 12 in
setting forth a famine in the land as the reason for the family's
migration, but it also explicitly requires us to recall the ch. 12
story by the notation: 'besides the former famine that was in
the days of Abraham' (26.1). No less directive for reading are
the more implicit connections, as when Yahweh says to Isaac,
'Do not go down to Egypt' (26.2), when Isaac has not shown
the slightest indication that he was thinking of going to Egypt,
but when we readers know—even if the characters have forgotten it—that, especially in wife-sister stories, patriarchs
always go down to Egypt when there is a famine in the land.
There is an equally explicit clue when the story says that Isaac
'went *to Abimelech* king of the Philistines Gerar-wards' (26.1;
RSV disguises the significant word-order, though NEB and NAB
preserve it); he does not just go, as we might have expected, '*to
Gerar*'—for that would simply have meant: 'to the city of
Gerar, where, as it happened, there was in the office of king a
certain Abimelech'. Rather, we are meant to recall that Isaac
has already been in Gerar before (embryonically in ch. 20)
and, more importantly, has been born within the boundaries of
the 'land' of Abimelech (cf. 20.15 with 21.31, 33-34), and has
set out from that same land for the incident on Mt Moriah (cf.

21.34 with 22.19). So he knows Abimelech already, if not personally then certainly from dinner-table conversation.[1]

Of more importance still is the 'mighty programmatic speech of promise'[2] that prefaces this chapter (26.2-5). In it the Abrahamic promise is repeated to Isaac, promises of 'all these lands', of 'multiply[ing] your descendants as the stars of heaven', and of blessing to all the nations of the earth through the patriarchs' descendants (26.3-4). But perhaps the most important narrative context for the story, at least for this story in comparison with the others, is that here the matriarch is not barren (not now, at any rate) and no children wait to be born to the parents. Already in ch. 25 Rebekah has given birth to Esau and Jacob, so we know immediately that here, whatever the danger may be, it cannot be to the promise of offspring. It is not the same danger.

Since nothing actually happens either to Isaac or to Rebekah, and no one acts upon the announcement that the wife is only a sister (Isaac is the only one who becomes sportive with her, 26.8), we may at first doubt that there is any real danger here at all. It is when we read Abimelech's words on discovering that she is Isaac's wife after all that we perceive that the danger which begins in the patriarch's head becomes in actuality a danger to the people of Gerar. 'What is this that you have done to us?', says the king. 'One of the people might easily have lain with your wife, and you would have brought guilt upon us' (26.10). However ungallant or outrageous may be Abimelech's casual assumption that if 'one of the people' (males, we presume) should take it into his head to lie with Rebekah, lain with she will be, the significant point is that the

---

1 By the time of Sarah's death (ch. 23) Abraham has moved back to Mamre, but Isaac is living at Beer-lahai-roi (24.62; 25.11), where he must still be when our story opens. Wherever that is, it is obviously south of Gerar, and probably on a route to Egypt—which is a further reason why Isaac might potentially think of escaping the famine in that direction. And in case anyone should be wondering whether this is the same Abimelech who figures in the Abraham story, we will not have far to read before we encounter Phicol (26.26; cf. 21.22), the very same troop-captain of what must surely be the very same Abimelech.

2 Von Rad, *Genesis*, p. 265.

king regards the seduction of the matriarch by any one of the
townsmen as a crime that would bring guilt upon 'us', the
people as a whole. In fact, he says, Isaac has already done the
people of Gerar a wrong in exposing them to the mere possibility of such a crime; the king uses the formal words of
indictment as he reproaches Isaac, 'What is this that you have
done to us?' (26.10).

It is the people who have been put at risk by Isaac's deception. The king himself has obviously not taken a fancy to
Rebekah, even though in her case it is the omniscient narrator
who has assured us that she is a beautiful woman (26.7),
whereas in 12.11 we had only the questionable testimony of
the ever devious Abraham to his wife's good looks. No,
Abimelech has clearly learned his lesson from the adventure
of ch. 20, and is not planning on 'sending' for *this* Hebrew's
wife. The only candidates for Rebekah's hand (supposing their
intentions to be so honourable) are 'the men of the place'
(26.7). Yet although the king himself is utterly innocent, even
of entertaining designs upon the matriarch, and is represented only as the outsider and onlooker, merely chancing
upon the happy couple 'exchanging conjugal caresses',[1]
*yitzchaq*ing about, we might say, 'sport' being the leitmotif of
Isaac's life,[2] Abimelech is stunned by the thought of the guilt
that could so easily have become attached to his people, the
fear too of who knows what divine catastrophe lurking in the
background. The role of the king in this narrative is no 'blind
motif', though the comparison with the much more obvious
acts of the king in the other two stories has led John van
Seters[3] and others to declare it so; rather, the function of the
king is to detect the true relation between Isaac and Rebekah
and so save his people from unintentional guilt.[4]

---

1 John Skinner, *A Critical and Exegetical Commentary on the Book
   of Genesis* (ICC; Edinburgh: T. & T. Clark, 1969), p. 364.
2 Derek Kidner, *Genesis* (TOTC; London: Tyndale Press, 1967), p.
   153.
3 John van Seters, *Abraham in History and Tradition* (London: Yale
   University Press, 1975), p. 180.
4 We saw in ch. 20, incidentally, the same sense in Abimelech of the
   whole people's implication in the wrongdoing of any individual:
   after he is warned by God that because he has taken Abraham's

The ancestor who brings danger

The story is not yet over with the detection of the deception, however. What we immediately discover is that from Abimelech's point of view the continued presence of Isaac in the territory of Gerar remains a danger for Abimelech's people. Something has to explain the extraordinary apodeictic warning by the king, who at first sight seems to be desperately over-reacting: 'Whoever touches this man or his wife shall surely be put to death' (26.11). While 'touching' a man often means striking him (is it implied that the people of Gerar will be strongly tempted to rough Isaac up for the danger he has brought them into?) and 'touching' a woman often means having intercourse with her, can the Gerarites be entirely sure, when a death penalty hangs over this 'touching', that the king does not mean *all* forms of touching? Are Isaac and his wife now in the position of the ritually unclean, people with whom it is dangerous to come into physical contact?

The long and short of it is that Isaac has proved to be the very opposite of a 'blessing' to the foreigners of Gerar. He has wished himself upon them, deceived them, brought potential guilt and actual danger upon them, leading their integrious king (cf. 20.6) to complain justifiably against him and put his own people under a threat of death if they associate with this Hebrew. Does this not mean that the patriarch whose descendants are grandly promised as a blessing to all the nations of the earth (26.4) is in this story nothing other, to be frank, than a curse? The conventional tale of the 'ancestor in danger' has become in this transformation a tale of 'the ancestor who brings danger'. The story, scorned on all sides today as naive, late, colourless, awkward, artificial, is actually a little master-piece in its own right, confounding all the expectations we brought to it from our reading of the previous wife-sister stories, but in a novel way presenting the ancestors as a threat of immense proportions to the promise under whose sign they ostensibly live.

If that had been the very end of the story, so much would

wife he himself is a 'dead man' (20.3) he responds, 'Lord, will you slay an innocent *people*?' (20.4).

have been clear. But this narrative, unlike the other two, has
no definite point of closure, and so invites us to consider its
significance further, in the light of subsequent events. That is
to say, the apparent resolution of the narrative, 'And Isaac
sowed in that land, and reaped in the same year a hundredfold' (26.12), is at the same time the exposition for the following narrative of the Philistine response to his wealth (26.12-
16); and thereafter all the little narrative units of this chapter
are chained on to one another.

What we read in the verses that follow is an ongoing narrative of the Hebrew patriarch as no blessing at all to the
Philistines—who are the only foreigners this patriarch has a
chance to practice his blessing on. The people of Gerar never
benefit from Isaac's presence or Isaac's wealth. We learn that
Isaac prospers enormously 'in that land', the land of the
Gerarites, be it noted, not in his own land, not in a land to
which he has been given title by divine fief; and he reaps a
hundredfold 'in the same year' as that of the famine he was
escaping from, Yahweh blessing him—but not, apparently,
blesing anyone else. He 'became rich, and gained more and
more until he became very wealthy' (26.13), but not so as to
overflow with blessings for his neighbours. The Philistines,
who are presumably not having so good a time as Isaac, not
surprisingly become 'envious' of him (26.14).

The upshot of Isaac's prosperity is that Abimelech ner-
vously begs him to 'go away from us, because you are so much
mightier than us' (26.16). Isaac complies, but he has not taken
the hint of how far distant Abimelech wishes him, for he
moves only as far as 'the valley of Gerar', which, wherever
precisely it is, cannot have been as far as Abimelech has had in
mind. Nor can he tumble to the fact that the reason why the
Philistines have been stopping up the wells that the herders of
Abraham once dug is not simple obstreperousness but because
they resent and feel threatened by the encroachment of the
Hebrew family upon their own grazing lands. So the little history of quarrels between the herdsmen of Gerar and Isaac's
herdsmen (26.18-22) is to be read as entirely of Isaac's making, and his smug announcement at the end that 'now
Yahweh has made room for us' (26.22) could have been made
much earlier if only he had realized that no one in Gerar was

thinking him quite as much God's gift to humanity as he was imagining himself.

The point of the closing episode of Abimelech's encounters with Isaac is really just the same. Abimelech feels himself threatened by Isaac, and wants to take out an insurance against the harm he fully expects will some day come his way from that quarter. 'We see plainly that Yahweh is with you', he confesses; 'so we say, let there be an oath between you and us ... that you will do us no harm' (26.28-29). Not the words of a Gentile who understands that he is to be the object of overflowing blessing from the Abrahamic family! Abimelech's justification for a non-aggression treaty is, interestingly enough, his own conviction that 'we', he and his people, have not in fact 'touched' (נגע, as in v. 11) Isaac. The further you can keep of out the way of the 'blessing to the nations' the safer it is for you, and if you are destined to be the recipient of the blessing it is wise to have a non-aggression pact with those who are supposed to be its channel! 'The foreign potentate has to acknowledge that Isaac is blessed by Yahweh', says Westermann,[1] and that can only be ironic if the context is the divine speech of vv. 2-5, where the blessing is designed to be not only for Isaac but also for the nations.

From this perspective we are almost compelled to wonder whether the re-phrasing of the divine promise in v. 24 may be more meaningful than at first appears. 'Fear not', says Yahweh, 'for I am with you and will bless you and will multiply your descendants.' Nothing more. Has the promise of blessing for the nations been silently abandoned under the circumstances? That thought may be a little extravagant, but the fact is that this element of the promise has in the present narrative of Isaac not only been in danger, but has been entirely lost sight of. It reminds us that in all these stories of the 'ancestor in danger', the danger the ancestor imagines for himself is of his own making, while the varying dangers his apprehension creates are always more serious.

What do we learn in addition from a second-time reading of this story? Not a lot if we are reading only as far as the end of Genesis. Which is an arbitrary and unsatisfying end, it must

---

1 Westermann, *Genesis 12–36,* p. 428.

be admitted. Read on, and you will find out what kind of a blessing Hebrews prove to be to Philistines, and how much Isaac's merely putting them in danger is to be preferred to Samson's slaying them hip and thigh or David's intermittent genocide of them throughout 2 Samuel. Which makes us wonder in the end whether Isaac was not by comparison quite a blessing—and whether we know any longer what a blessing is. At which point we lay down our pens and call in the deconstructionists.

Chapter 4

THE OLD TESTAMENT HISTORIES:
A READER'S GUIDE[*]

What, according to the Old Testament, happened in history?
So much of the Old Testament is historiographical that it is
essential that we as readers should have a clear grasp of what
is the broad sweep of its story of the past. We do not need to
know only what the historiographical narratives tell us in de-
tail, but also, and even more importantly, what their function
is and what view of the past they are presenting.

1. *Definitions*

Two preliminary definitional questions need airing; they cannot, unfortunately, be settled, but it is better to raise them than
to ignore them. They are: What is the Old Testament? and,
Which are the historiographical books?

Since our concern here is with the Old Testament, and not
simply with the Hebrew Bible, we must take proper cognizance of the fact that the Old Testament has included different books in different orders to different people at different
times. Or at least, so as not to cast the issue in so programmatically historical a fashion, we should acknowledge that at the
present time the Old Testament exists in several different
forms. The principal difference lies between the Catholic
tradition which includes the Deuterocanonical books and the
Protestant tradition—parallel to the Jewish tradition—which

---

[*] This Chapter is a significantly revised and in some respects ex-
tended version of my earlier piece, 'Introduction to the Biblical
Story: Genesis–Esther', in the volume produced by members of the
Society of Biblical Literature, *Harper's Bible Commentary*, ed.
James L. Mays (San Francisco: Harper and Row, 1988), pp. 74-84.

excludes them as Apocrypha.[1] Intermediate between these traditions is that of the Church of England and the Anglican communion, which *includes* in its Old Testament the Apocryphal books, but isolates them from the Hebrew books of the Old Testament and collects them in a group of their own following the Hebrew books. The Protestant and Anglican Apocrypha includes in addition two historiographical books not found within the Catholic Deuterocanonicals, viz. 1 and 2 Esdras (known as 3 and 4 Esdras to Catholics who use the names 1 and 2 Esdras for Ezra and Nehemiah).[2]

Clearly the question, Which Old Testament?, is fundamental to any discussion of its historiographical books. But there is no 'right' answer, and there is no 'objective' solution to the conundrum, Which Old Testament? Would-be readers often find themselves compelled willy-nilly to adopt the position of one or another of the rival 'interpretative communities' before they can even get started reading seriously or before they can even understand what the debate is all about. There is certainly no easy solution to be found in the term 'Hebrew Bible'; for while it is true that the standard, current, Hebrew Bible contains the same books as the Protestant Old Testament, there is no reason to think that has always been the case. For some books that are no longer extant in Hebrew were once 'biblical' books in Hebrew, and the Jews who translated the Bible into Greek in the second century BCE included in their Septuagint translation some such books as well as others which had never been in Hebrew. So the language of a book has never been a sufficient determinant for canonical status, and the Jewish view of the contents of the Bible has been more diverse than is often recognized. The differences between Catholics and Protestants are in fact very largely the same

1 Protestant Bibles prior to 1827 in fact included the Apocrypha, but I refer here to the prevailing situation at the present day. There are many complications: the RSV, for example, is in origin a Protestant Bible (there was a Catholic edition of it in 1966), but one of the forms in which it is published includes the Apocrypha. What does that make the RSV?

2 The Protestant and Anglican Apocrypha also includes The Prayer of Manasseh, which is not in the Catholic canon; but it is not a historiographical book.

differences as existed between Greek-speaking and Hebrew-speaking Jews.

The second question is, Which are the historiographical books? Here there is even more uncertainty, since such a classification has no ecclesiastical tradition to support it, and scholars—even those loyal to some church or other religious community—are free to make their own decisions as may seem right in their own eyes. No one will dispute that Ruth is one such book, beginning as it does, 'In the days when the judges ruled there was a famine in the land ...', and continuing by recounting a story set in that historical period. Not many, however, will allow that the book beginning, 'The vision of Isaiah the son of Amoz, which he saw concerning Judah and Jerusalem in the days of Uzziah, Jotham, Ahaz, and Hezekiah, kings of Judah', should be so called, even though it contains reports of what is supposed to have been said in those years as well as chapters (36–39) of straightforward historiographical narrative. Presumably the reason—perhaps the only reason —why Isaiah is not said to be an historiographical work is because it has already been pigeonholed to another category, prophecy. The example highlights the degree of arbitrariness that attaches to any attempt to categorize the books of the Old Testament. Nevertheless, the attempt has to be made if we are to be able to think sensibly about Old Testament 'histories' and make meaningful observations about their view of the past and their function.

Shall we agree, then, for the sake of this discussion, that the 'historiographical' books of the Old Testament can consist of the following, given the broadest definition of the 'Old Testament'?

Genesis	2 Samuel
Exodus	1 Kings
Leviticus	2 Kings
Numbers	1 Chronicles
Deuteronomy	2 Chronicles
Joshua	Ezra
Judges	Nehemiah
Ruth	Esther
1 Samuel	Daniel

1 Esdras	Azariah and the
2 Esdras	Song of the Three
Tobit	Young Men
Judith	Susanna
Baruch	Bel and the Dragon
Letter of Jeremiah	1 Maccabees
The Prayer of	2 Maccabees

The order of the above list is of course not a random one, but plainly reflects a certain canonical tradition. It is, in fact, the order of the Revised Standard Version, in one of its two forms.[1] It is not, of course, the order of the Hebrew Bible in its standard printed editions; for quite apart from the presence of the apocryphal books, it differs from the Hebrew Bible in having Ruth follow Judges and in having 1 Chronicles, 2 Chronicles, Ezra, Nehemiah rather than the order Ezra, Nehemiah, 1 Chronicles, 2 Chronicles.

Unless one is a reader committed to obedience to the details of one canonical tradition, there is nothing sacrosanct about any particular order of the books. There is nothing to stop a reader finding one order 'better' than another or rearranging books on some different principle than that used by the framers of a particular canon (if such could be known). There cannot be many readers who will not agree that the order 1 Chronicles, 2 Chronicles, Ezra, Nehemiah is 'better' than the Hebrew Bible order, since it is a fundamental—and reasonable—expectation of readers that chronicle-like accounts will be told in more or less chronological order, and such a principle of arrangement can hardly be allowed to be subverted by the ordering principle used in the Hebrew Bible (whatever it was). Not all readers will be so sure that it is best to make Ruth follow Judges, and some might argue that it would be better to collect books that interrupt the main flow of a connected history into an appendix rather than interpose them in settings where they admittedly belong by chronological right. No matter the rights and wrongs of these particular issues; the point is simply that readers have the right to arrange books in any order that makes sense to them. In fact, readers are ex-

1 The Prayer of Azariah and the Song of the Three Young Men constitute additions to the book of Daniel, and would follow Dan. 3.23.

ercising such a right all the time: whenever they decide to
read one book first and another book second, they are making
their own order. And who can forbid readers to do that?
What order, then, would I be arguing in the present study to
be a meaningful one, worthy of consideration by other readers
also—which is to say, not merely the whim of this particular
reader?

To my mind, the most important structuring and ordering
principle for the historiographical books of the Old Testament
lies in the existence of two major distinct story sequences,
which I call the Primary History and the Secondary History.[1]
These two Histories correspond to what has conventionally
been known as the Pentateuch plus the Deuteronomistic
History on the one hand, and the Chronicler's History
(including the books of Ezra and Nehemiah) on the other. All
the other historiographical books of the Old Testament may be
attached more or less loosely, by token of their subject matter,
to one or other of these unified narratives. We can thus designate two blocks of historiographical books, partly consisting of
and partly attached to, these major Histories.

To the first block, which contains the Primary History and
two other books, belong:

---

1 As far as I know, the term 'Primary History' was first used by D.N.
   Freedman in his article, 'Deuteronomic History, The', in *The
   Interpreter's Dictionary of the Bible. Supplementary Volume*, ed.
   K. Crim (Nashville: Abingdon, 1976), pp. 226-28; cf. also his 'The
   Earliest Bible', in Michael P. O'Connor and D.N. Freedman (eds.),
   Backgrounds for the Bible (Winona Lake, IN: Eisenbrauns, 1987),
   pp. 29-37; and Edward L. Greenstein, *Essays on Biblical Method
   and Translation* (Brown Judaic Studies, 92; Atlanta: Scholars
   Press, 1989), p. 12. The term Octateuch was used in the early
   church for the eight books, Genesis–Judges plus Ruth, but no
   large-scale implications were derived from the term. In the older
   scholarship the term Enneateuch was by analogy applied to the historical corpus of Genesis–2 Kings (excluding Ruth), but the focus
   here was always upon the presumed sources of these books rather
   upon the shape and significance of them considered as a whole; cf.
   O. Eissfeldt, *The Old Testament. An Introduction* (tr. Peter R. Ackroyd; Oxford: Basil Blackwell, 1966), pp. 134-36, 156.

Genesis	1 Samuel
Exodus	2 Samuel
Leviticus	1 Kings
Numbers	2 Kings
Deuteronomy	Ruth
Joshua	Tobit
Judges	

In this block, the Primary History itself consists of a self-contained and uninterrupted narrative in eleven books down to 2 Kings, with two further more loosely attached works, which may be termed pendants. Ruth positions itself very clearly 'in the days when the judges ruled' (1.1), while Tobit is explicitly connected with the captivity of the northern kingdom by the Assyrian Shalmaneser (1.1-2), an event we read of only in the Primary History (2 Kgs 17.5-6).

To the second block, which contains the four books of the Secondary History and eleven other words, there belong the following books:[1]

1 Chronicles	1 Esdras
2 Chronicles	2 Esdras
Ezra	Judith
Nehemiah	Baruch
Esther (in its shorter	Letter of Jeremiah
and longer forms)	Susanna
Daniel (with or without	Bel and the Dragon
The Prayer of Azariah &	1 Maccabees
the Song of the Three Young Men)	2 Maccabees

Here 1 Chronicles, 2 Chronicles, Ezra, and Nehemiah clearly form a unified narrative sequence.[2] To this Secondary History 1 and 2 Maccabees somewhat self-consciously attach themselves with their opening reference to the defeat of 'Darius, king of the Persians and the Medes' by Alexander the Great (1 Macc. 1.1), Darius being a prominent figure in the later chapters of the Secondary History (cf. Ezr. 4.4, 24; 5.6–6.16). Daniel is presumably to be located with this sequence of

1 The Letter of Jeremiah is frequently regarded as ch. 6 of the book of Baruch.
2 Nothing is being said here about the historical origins of the books or whether they have a common authorship; it is simply a question of their narrative sequence.

books, since it opens with the notice of the removal of temple vessels to Babylonia by Nebuchadnezzar in the time of Jehoiachim (1.1-2), an event which 2 Chronicles knows of (36.7) but 2 Kings does not (cf. 23.34–24.7). 1 and 2 Esdras, through their involvement with the person of Ezra, are evidently connected with the post-exilic narratives of the Secondary History. The book of Judith also is plainly enough set in post-exilic times, since the 'people of Israel' are all living 'in Judaea' and have 'only recently returned from the captivity' (4.1, 3)—even though the name of the villain of the piece is given as 'Nebuchadnezzar, who ruled over the Assyrians' (1.1)! Baruch and the Letter of Jeremiah could in principle be attached to either the Primary or the Secondary History, but the latter location seems preferable because of the marked presence of Jeremiah in its material dealing with the exile to Babylonia (2 Chron. 36.12, 21, 22; Ezr. 1.1). Susanna and Bel and the Dragon must of course be connected with the book of Daniel, since he is involved in both narratives.

I conclude that it is useful to discriminate between two *blocks* of historiographical books in the Old Testament (understood in the widest sense of that term), and within those blocks two *histories* or narrative sequences. Most of what follows in this Chapter concerns the histories rather than the blocks; the distinction between blocks and histories is not one of kind, however, but rather rests on a formal consideration, the degree of tightness of the narrative connection between books.

2. The Two Histories in General

I have suggested that it possible, and in fact desirable, in the interests of a coherent view of what the Old Testament represents as going on in the past, to think of the historiographical books of the Old Testament as belonging to two major blocks which centre around two distinct and major historical narratives. I turn now to examine these two story sequences, which are alike in many ways but which also show surprising and important differences. Each sequence begins with the creation of the world and goes on to recount some of the history of the Hebrew people. But the two sequences conclude at very different points in the history: the Primary History concludes with the end of the Judaean kingdom at the fall of Jerusalem in 587 BCE, and the Secondary History finishes in the fifth century BCE with the establishment of post-exilic Judaea as a province of the Persian empire.

The different points of conclusion are not the only sign that the two Histories have fundamentally different outlooks on the past. For whereas the Primary History consistently stresses elements of decline, disaster, and failure in the national history, the Secondary History emphasizes positive aspects. The two Histories thus represent alternative ways of recounting the past, and in so doing problematize the past for all their readers. For the Old Testament itself simply juxtaposes the two Histories, without offering any hermeneutical key to their dual existence, nor even any historical key to their comparative value for the reconstruction of the history of the Jewish people. That is to say, the Old Testament does not tell us how we are to esteem either of the works when we find them offering us two differing accounts of the past, nor how we are to imagine the history of Israel 'actually' proceeded.

From the reader's point of view, while it is possible to turn over to professional historians the detailed questions about the accuracy or validity of the accounts of the two Histories, a major question still remains regarding the significance of our having within the Old Testament two 'authorized' versions of the past which differ markedly from each other. Necessarily, readers of the Biblical text are not only invited but required, by this circumstance, to make their own assessment of the meaning of the fact that the two divergent Histories both exist. In so doing readers cannot avoid re-examining their own notions of what constitutes success or failure in history; or, if they are reading within some religious perspective, they cannot help themselves re-evaluating what it is that constitutes blessing or curse, or what it is that can be assessed as promise and as fulfilment. All of that means to say that readers cannot interpret these works without some degree of personal involvement or without engaging in some kind of ideological or theological reflection.

3. *The Primary History (Genesis–2 Kings)*

What may be said of the Primary History as a whole? If, as readers, we do not simply plunge into it at Genesis 1, opting for a purely linear reading of the work from beginning to end, but ask after the structure of the entire work, some major structural aspects soon become visible. For within narrative of the Primary History there are some obvious milestones, significant moments in the national life, marking out a periodization of the History. The death of Moses, who has been the key human figure in the narrative from Exodus to Deuteronomy, is clearly one such crucial event, occurring as it does on the eve of the Israelite entry into the promised land. The opening of the Book of Joshua, 'After the death of Moses ...', signals that transition, and at the same time provides a model for other major transitions in the History. Thus Judges begins 'After the death of Joshua', 2 Samuel 'After the death of Saul', and 2 Kings 'After the death of Ahab' (though in this case the transition seems much less significant). 1 Kings is a little out of step, in that it begins just *before* the death of David; nevertheless, it remains true that the death of that hero of the story is a major transitional moment in the narrative; it is just that David is a long time dying (1 Kgs 1.1; 2.1, 10-11). Structurally, then the Primary History may be said to be arranged around the lifetimes of important individuals: the Patriarchs (Genesis), Moses (Exodus–Deuteronomy), Joshua (Joshua), the Judges (Judges), Samuel and Saul (1 Samuel), David (2 Samuel), Solomon, Elijah, Ahab (1 Kings), the other kings (2 Kings).

Such an analysis does not take us very far, however. For it has regard only to the *content* of the narrative. If we were to ask after the *point* of the narrative or the ideological statement competent readers of the narrative are likely to find it making, we might say something like this. The narrative of the Primary History is one of fair beginnings and foul endings. Not only at the beginning of the work but at several key moments throughout the course of it, there are positive and promising signs of how the history is going to develop. In repeated instances, however, and in its global direction, the history tells of the disappointment of hopes.

The first of the fair beginnings we encounter in the promise of Genesis 12 to Abraham that his descendants—the Israelite people—will be vastly numerous, that they will inhabit a land of their own, that they will be the object of divine blessing, and that they will be a blessing to other nations. Yet by the time we have read to the end of 2 Kings we have seen that these promises have ultimately failed of attainment, even though there have been signals of their potential success along the way. The narrative facts are that, by the end of the narrative sequence, ten of the twelve tribes of Israel have long ago been lost to view in Assyrian captivity and the remainder have just now been submerged in Babylonian exile. And Judah has been 'taken into exile out of its land' (2 Kgs 25.21), it has 'come to the point' that Yahweh has 'cast them [Jerusalem and Judah] out of his presence' (24.19), while what the nations of the world have experienced from Israel is not in the least a blessing but either military domination (when Israel ruled an empire) or else insubordination (when Israel formed part of the Assyrian or Babylonian empires).

Fair beginnings are also announced by the various styles of leadership Israel experiences in the Primary History. Every type of leader—warrior, judge, king and prophet—though represented at the first as Yahweh's gift to the nation proves in the end either disastrous or at least ineffectual. Moses the warrior-leader of the people can guide them to the promised land, but not into it because of his own personal failure; he can bring them divine law but he cannot prevent the curses of Deuteronomy 28 falling upon them if they fail to be obedient. Joshua the warrior, whom no man is supposed to be able to withstand in his fight for territory for his people (Josh. 1.5) and whose function is to gain the land of Canaan as a possession for the Hebrews (1.6, 15), is to be found, at the end of his days, still finding it necessary to stiffen the resolve of his countrymen against 'the nations that remain' (23.4) and to urge them to remain loyal to the worship of Yahweh rather than 'the gods of the Amorites in whose land you dwell' (24.15). The land is still the land of the Amorites'!

The history of the judges, who are 'raised up' by God (Judg. 2.16), likewise reads as a story of decline, from the first and unexceptionable judge Othniel upon whom the spirit of

Yahweh comes and who thereupon can overcome an oppressive 'king of Mesopotamia' (3.10), to Samson, whom also the spirit of Yahweh 'stirs' (13.25), but who—unlike other judges—cannot bring 'rest' to his nation, and who cannot control the Philistine threat any more than he can control his own appetites, but must suffer the indignity of having his era denoted 'the days of the Philistines' (15.20).

Or if it is Samuel rather than Samson who is to be regarded as the last of the judges, we cannot help observing how conspicuously he fails to fulfil his boyhood promise as purveyor of the word of Yahweh (1 Sam. 3), appointing his unscrupulous sons as his successors to the judgeship (8.1-3), and resisting the evident intention of Yahweh to institute a monarchy (e.g. 8.22).

The monarchy as an institution, we next note, holds out great promise, but it too very soon proves its potential for disaster. The first king, Saul, chosen by divinely directed lot (1 Sam. 10.20-24), is very soon 'rejected ... from being king over Israel' (15.26), Yahweh having 'repented' that he has made Saul king (15.11). The most esteemed of Israel's kings, David, is condemned out of his own mouth, sinning against Yahweh in the matter of Bathsheba and Uriah (2 Sam. 12.13) and in the numbering of the people (24.10). Though he is promised that his line will rule over Israel 'for ever' (7.13, 16), he is also threatened with a prophecy that his dynasty will 'never' be free from feuds and attacks (12.10).

The narrative of the monarchy continues with David's son Solomon, who begins his reign by 'loving' Yahweh (1 Kgs 3.3) and building him a temple (1 Kgs 6–7), but in the end proves to be 'not wholly true to the LORD his God' (11.4) and is told that Yahweh will 'surely tear the kingdom from [him]' (11.11). In consequence, Solomon's son Rehoboam loses the allegiance of all the tribes except Judah (12.19-20) and Jeroboam his northern rival institutes unlicensed sanctuaries, which become 'a sin to the house of Jeroboam, so as to cut it off and to destroy it from the face of the earth' (13.34). In the northern kingdom the kings regularly follow the example of Jeroboam and lead their people into sin; Omri, for example, 'walked in all the way of Jeroboam the son of Nebat, and in the sins which he made Israel to sin, provoking the LORD, the God of Israel, to anger'

(16.26) In the southern kingdom, two kings are wholeheartedly approved of by Yahweh: Hezekiah (2 Kgs 18.6), who nevertheless is the first to hear of the forthcoming exile to Babylon (20.16-19), and Josiah (22.2; 23.25), who nevertheless is killed in battle (23.29-30) despite a prophecy that he will be 'gathered to [his] grave in peace' (22.20). Several others receive qualified praise, but of six of the last seven kings of Judah it is uniformly reported that they 'did what was evil in the sight of the LORD' (e.g. 21.2).

The other institution of leadership in Israel is that of the prophets. They appear at various times in the course of the narrative, from Moses (Deut. 34.10) who functions both as Yahweh's mouthpiece and as an intercessor for the people, through anonymous prophets in the period of the judges (Judg. 6.8-10; cf. 2.1-3; 10.11-14), bands of prophets in the time of Samuel (1 Sam. 10.5) and schools of 'the sons of the prophets' in the time of Elisha, to the famous individual prophets Samuel, Nathan, Elijah and Elisha. As a channel of communication between the divine and the human, the prophets hold greater promise than any of the other leaders, but nonetheless they are remarkably ineffectual: quite apart from the more trivial tasks of divination prophets are called upon to perform (like finding lost animals, 1 Sam. 9), their success in influencing national history proves to be minimal. Disobedience to Yahweh's word as delivered by a prophet, it is true, is very early on recognized as a fatal crime for a king: Saul is 'rejected' from being king because he has rejected the 'word' of Yahweh through Samuel (1 Sam. 15.23). Elsewhere, on the whole, however, the prophetic word does no more than announce a doom-laden future which is not open to adjustment (e.g. Ahijah's prophecy in 1 Kgs 14.7-11) but which merely wakens echoes of the original prophecy as it comes to pass (cf. 15.29; also 2 Kgs 9.25-26, 36; 10.10, 17). In the large stretch of the narrative given over to the activity of the prophets Elijah and Elisha (1 Kings 17–2 Kings 10) there is indeed an outstandingly successful confrontation between the prophet of Yahweh and those prophets of Baal that are supported by the royal court (1 Kings 18); nevertheless it is not the prophet Elijah but the king Jehu who most decisively defends the worship of Yahweh when he 'wipe[s] out Baal from Israel'

(10.28), which is to say, from the nation as a whole. Prophets are indeed found designating future kings by unction (1 Sam. 10.1; 2 Kgs 9.1-10), but prophets do not make kings; it needs popular acclamation (1 Sam. 10.24–11.15) or a coup d'état (2 Kgs 9.11-37) to achieve real political ends.

This downhill direction of the Primary History, towards national decline and the negation of national hopes that had been entertained at the beginning of the story, was, now we come to recognize it, already foreshadowed by the opening chapters of Genesis. In Genesis 1–11, the Primeval History, fair beginnings for the human race—before ever the scope of the narrative will be narrowed down to the Abrahamic family—are very soon tarnished by human perversity. The primal couple are expelled from the garden in no time at all (3.23), the first brother becomes the first murderer (4.8), the multiplication of humankind is accompanied by a corresponding increase in human wickedness (6.1, 5), and, at Babel, the first co-operative endeavour in human history leads immediately to a permanent 'scattering' of the race across the face of the earth (11.9). Against that background it is perhaps not surprising that the focus on the Abrahamic family from Genesis 12 onwards should reveal, not some undoing of the primeval tragedy, but, rather, a long drawn-out replay of it. There is not a lot of difference between Gen. 6.5-7, near the History's beginning, and 2 Kgs 17.18-23, near its end: at the time of the flood, when God sees that humankind's thoughts are 'only evil continually', he is sorry that he created them, and determines to 'blot' them out from the face of the ground by a great flood; at the time of the exile, things are not so very different when the Israelite people over many generations have done 'wicked things, provoking the LORD to anger' (2 Kgs 17.11), and he now 'removes' or 'casts' them 'out of his sight' (17.18, 20, 23). The greatest difference between the Primaeval History and the rest of the Primary History is that in Genesis 1–11 every episode of human sin followed by divine punishment contains a further element of mitigation of the punishment; Adam and Eve, for example, though expelled from the garden, do not actually die in the day they eat of the fruit, and Cain, though driven out from the tillable earth to be a fugitive, carries a divine mark of protection against any who might seek to slay him. In the remainder of the History as a whole, however, there is no mitigation, either realized or envisaged, of the fate of the Israelite people.

Or is there? Some have thought that the concluding paragraph of 2 Kings (25.27-30) recounting the release from prison in Babylon of the ex-king Jehoiachin of Judah, injects a note of hope on the very last page of the History, hinting perhaps that Jehoiachin's good fortune may be one day be that of the entire people. It is true that Jehoiachin is given a royal pension and dines at the Babylonian king's table, at 'a seat above the seats of the kings who were with him in Babylon' (25.28); but it is also true that Jehoiachin has spent 37 years in prison in Babylon (twice the time he had lived in Judah; cf. 24.8), that even with his dining rights he is still effectively a prisoner in the Babylonian court, that his pension is humiliatingly paid to him on a daily basis, and that at the time of the writing of the Primary History Jehoiachin is apparently already dead (cf. 25.30: 'a regular allowance was given him by the king ... as long as he lived'). None of this augurs well for the Jewish people, nor can this admittedly undisastrous conclusion reverse the downhill direction in which the whole of the Primary History has been moving.[1]

---

1 On the ideology of the Pentateuch and of the Deuteronomistic History as wholes, see, for example, David J.A. Clines, *The Theme of the Pentateuch* (JSOTSup, 10; Sheffield: JSOT Press, 1978); Robert Polzin, *Moses and the Deuteronomist. A Literary Study of the Deuteronomic History, Part One: Deuteronomy, Joshua, Judges* (New York: Seabury, 1980); and *Samuel and the Deuteronomist. A Literary Study of the Deuteronomistic History, Part Two: 1 Samuel* (San Francisco: Harper & Row, 1989); Martin Noth, *The Deuteronomistic History* (tr. Jane Doull *et al.*; JSOTSup, 15; Sheffield: JSOT Press, 1981 [original edition: *Überlieferungsgeschichtliche Studien* (Schriften der Königsberger Gelehrten Gesellschaft. Geisteswissenschaftliche Klasse, 18; Halle: Max Niemeyer Verlag, 1943), pp. 1-110); Frank Moore Cross, *Canaanite Myth and Hebrew Epic. Essays in the History of the Religion of Israel* (Cambridge, MA: Harvard University Press, 1973), chap. 4 'Kings and Prophets', pp. 217-90.

4. *The Secondary History*

The Secondary History begins with the creation of the world, as does the Primary History; but it carries the story of the Israelite people much further, beyond the exile to the Persian period of the fifth century BCE. By comparison with the Primary History, the Secondary History is remarkable for its omission of any narrative for the period from the creation down to the death of Saul (1 Chron. 10)—genealogies fill the narrative gap—and for its exclusion of the history of the northern kingdom. Clearly the first crucial event in this History is not the Exodus or Conquest, but the reign of David and the establishment of his dynasty. In this History, David does not first rule over Judah and then extend his power over the northern tribes (cf. 2 Sam. 5.5); he is made king by 'all Israel' from the beginning (1 Chron. 11.1).

The importance of David in the Secondary History is that he is represented as the institutor of the Israelite system of worship, especially of the temple, which is his idea and which he instructs his son Solomon to build (1 Chron. 17; 22). The Levites also, who actually perform the worship of the temple, are appointed by David (1 Chron. 23–26). Nothing is said of David's misdemeanours, and even the narrative of his exploits as a warrior seems to be included only by way of introduction to the story of his bringing the ark, as the focus of the worship of Yahweh, to Jerusalem (1 Chron. 13).

The section of the history devoted to Solomon likewise has as its theme Solomon as the builder of the temple (2 Chron. 1–9). Here too any negative aspects of the king's personality are passed over (contrast 1 Kgs 2.1–3.1). Later kings of Judah are not indeed depicted in the Secondary History as uniformly righteous, but special emphasis is given to those who effect religious reforms or repair the temple: Asa (2 Chron. 15), Jehoshaphat (19.4-11), Joash (24.4-14), Hezekiah (29.3–31.23), and Josiah (34.1–35.19). The history of the monarchy in this Secondary History thus seems to be primarily a history of the establishment and maintenance of the worship of God; the function of kings is primarily to promote correct and lavish worship, and the function of the people is provide the necessary funds and personnel for the temple services.

In the post-exilic segment of the Secondary History in Ezra and Nehemiah the same interest is very evident. The return from exile in Babylonia is authorized by the Persian king Cyrus specifically in order to rebuild the Jerusalem temple (Ezr. 1.2), and the first action of the returned exiles is to rebuild the temple altar 'in its place' (3.3) and to reinstitute sacrifices there, even before the temple itself has been rebuilt. The first major climax of these books is the completion of the temple building 'by command of the God of Israel and by decree of Cyrus and Darius and Artaxerxes king of Persia' (6.14), followed by the celebration of the traditional festivals (6.19-22). Other important moments in the narrative are the elimination of foreigners from the worshipping community (Ezr. 10), the securing of the city and its people by the enclosure of a wall (Neh. 3–4; 12.27-43), instruction in the law of Yahweh (ch. 8), and cultic reforms (ch. 13). Nehemiah's closing words are in the closest harmony with this History's primary interest: 'I established the duties of the priests and Levites, each in his work; and I provided for the wood offering, at appointed times, and for the first fruits' (13.30-31). And Nehemiah is not even a professional religious man, but a Jewish official in the Persian civil service.

So the entire Secondary History concludes on an upbeat note. It harmonizes well with the outlook of the narrative as a whole, that the purpose for which history has existed is the worship of God, and the people of Israel, aided by the right-living kings of Judah, have in fact throughout the only history worth writing about been carrying out that worship faithfully and joyfully. This quite different perspective on national history from that of the Primary History is particularly well illustrated by the way the two Histories handle the question of the meaning of the exile. For 2 Kings the exile is a punishment for national iniquity, an unredeemed disaster, and the endpoint of the whole narrative. But for 2 Chronicles the exile is punishment for a cultic offence, the pollution of the temple (36.14), it is destined to come to an end at a time predicted by the prophet Jeremiah (36.21; cf. Jer. 25.11; 29.10), and it is no kind of end; for the book concludes not with the exile but with an announcement of the plans of Cyrus to rebuild the temple (36.22-23).

5. *The Reception of the Two Histories*

The understanding that I have just now presented of the Old
Testament as containing two competing historical narratives
does not correspond, it needs to be said, with the way in which
these historiographical books have been usually understood by
the communities that have preserved them. This is because it
has not been customary to look at ancient sacred books as literary works that generate meaning through their overall
shape, their structure, and their dominant tendencies, that is,
through their identity as wholes. These books, like the other
Biblical books, have tended rather to be valued piecemeal for
their diverse contents.

Thus the Primary History has been understood both in the
Jewish and the Christian communities as containing law and
history. It does, of course. In Exodus to Deuteronomy there is
an imposing collection of ancient Israelite legal texts, unparalleled elsewhere in the Old Testament, which remains essential
for the moral and legal beliefs and practices of Jews today.
Christians have generally tried to discriminate between the
moral laws of these books, which they have considered as
having some kind of divine authorization, and the more
strictly ritual laws, which they have regarded as applicable
only to the Jewish people. These interpretations, both Jewish
and Christian, whether or not they have a validity, ignore the
fact that the laws of the Primary History are *narrated*, i.e. set
in a narrative context. It would be more appropriate, therefore, to understand them—even the Ten Commandments—
not as laws claiming universal truth but as texts that will
become meaningful only as they are understood within the
narrative framework that surrounds them.

The Primary History also contains a valuable collection of
historical materials. In fact, for most of the period it covers, it is
the only source we have for knowing anything at all about
what actually happened in ancient Israel. But it is plain from
the structure of the History that its concern is not primarily
historiographical in the sense of recording the events of the
past. The narrative has an argument or a thesis it wishes to
establish; and since that thesis concerns the religious meaning

of the total historical period that it describes our primary approach to understanding of the narrative should be a literary one that focuses upon the ideological character of the text.

If it is true that the Primary History has been plundered for its contents rather than regarded as a unified work with a distinctive thesis, it is even more true of the Secondary History that its significance as a whole has been largely ignored. Ever since the Septuagint translation in the second century BCE of 1 and 2 Chronicles under the heading Paraleipomena, 'the omitted things', Chronicles has been regarded as little more than a supplement to Samuel and Kings rather than as presenting a distinctive view of the past and indeed of the purpose of creation. Ezra and Nehemiah, for their part, have been treated more as a continuation of the history of Genesis–2 Kings carried forward into post-exilic times than as further evidence for the argument of Chronicles.

A further effect of regarding the narratives as essentially history is the following. Both Jewish and Christian readers have always known that the history of Israel did not really come to an end with the exile or with the post-exilic age. So the particular point at which the two Biblical Histories conclude has seemed arbitrary to them and therefore meaningless. So, for example, the fact that the historical sequence Genesis–2 Kings concludes in the exile and recounts no story of the return has seemed a matter of indifference; for the *facts* are known from elsewhere, and what matters are the facts. By contrast, if we now recognize the existence of the two sequences of narratives as literary works in their own right we are inevitably led into a reassessment of the Old Testament's view of the past, and to an uncovering of a conflict and dissension that has been cloaked over.

So long as the narratives have been thought to contribute to a programme other than their own—such as laying down the laws by which to live or providing information about the events of the past—their truly challenging and subversive nature has lain unremarked. This is not surprising, for the communities that have preserved them have always been in the business of conservation, of themselves no less than of their sacred books. Once we acknowledge that the Old Testament contains in these two historical sequences two divergent ways of remembering the past we become obliged to make decisions for ourselves, not so much about the relative historical worth of each of the Histories (unless we happen to be technically trained historians), but about whether, or to what extent, it is possible to regard as scriptures texts that contain so much tension within themselves. There is no obviously or objectively correct decision; the reader has to make personal decisions and take personal responsibility for them. As I have suggested, the history of the Bible's reception, even by groups that have esteemed it highly, is, to a very considerable extent, a chronicle of misapprehensions of the Bible. And so readers who read for themselves and have given up having texts read to them and for them are not reading only 'for themselves' but also, inevitably, *against others.*

6. *The Reader's Revenge*

After all this talk of texts being misapprehended by readers, we return to the reality of actual readers and the politics of reading. The fact of the matter is that, however powerful texts may be, readers are more powerful. In any contest between texts and readers, readers are always going to win. For readers have in their hands the life of the text. If a text is going to be opened, it will be a reader who decides that. If it is to be shut, or ignored, or misapprehended, or read out of order or upside down, readers will do whatever they choose to do. Even if the readers do not really know what they are doing to their texts, they will be doing it all the same—and getting away with it. Such are the risks texts run by lying around on shelves and tables.

So if readers—despite the intentions of authors and the structure of literary works and their ideological stances— insist on reading the biblical histories their way, there is nothing that can be done about it. There might even be something to be said for it. Must we indeed require readers of the Primary History to keep firmly out of their minds throughout their reading one major fact extrinsic to the work, namely, that the exile of the Judaeans was not the end of the Hebrew people, and that a return (of sorts) to the land and a reconstitution of the community took place half a century after the

point reached at the end of 2 Kings? Is it indeed possible for
readers, even with the most respectful attitude to the text, to
hold in abeyance for ever their knowledge which they have
gained from outside the text, knowledge which the text has not
divulged to them, and of which the text itself is probably
unaware? They will have been accustomed, when watching a
film or reading a novel that was proving too painful to them, to
break frame and remind themselves that it is only a fiction;
perhaps they have even trained themselves to wake up out of
disturbing nightmares saying, It's only a dream. How long,
then, can they go on suspending their disbelief in the stance of
the Primary History, for example, which is to say, *pretending*
that the end of the story indeed coincided with the historical
end of the Hebrew people?

Does not the flow of historical events, in short, militate
against the statement that the Primary History as a whole is
making? And what exactly is wrong with reading Ezra–
Nehemiah as the *sequel* to the narrative of Genesis to 2 Kings?
The fact that the author of the Primary History did not intend
it—even that the author of the Secondary History and of
Ezra–Nehemiah itself did not intend it—is beside the point.
What is so wrong with listening to Mozart's *Requiem* with
Sussmayr's additions?[1] What, for that matter, is to stop us
regarding the Secondary History not as an *alternative* way of
telling the history of Israel, but as a *corrective* to an unduly
pessimistic Primary History? And what, in the end, justifies
calling Genesis–2 Kings the *Primary* History? Is that not
already to prejudge the question of the relationship of the
Histories? And, in the end, *are* there *two* histories, or is that
also a matter of the readers' decision? Whatever stands writ-

---

1 'We need not concern ourselves with the rest of the work', wrote
  Alfred Einstein after he had treated the authentically Mozartian
  elements of the *Requiem Mass in D Minor*, 'since it originated with
  Süssmayr; only for the *Benedictus* did Süssmayr apparently have
  an indication of Mozart's intentions' (*Mozart. His Character, His
  Work* [tr. Arthur Mendel and Nathan Broder; London: Cassell,
  1946], p. 354). The fact is, however, that my record of the music—
  like most people's—undiscriminatingly includes Süssmayr's
  Sanctus, *Benedictus*, and *Agnus Dei*, and I 'concern myself' with
  the whole work, including the non-Mozartian elements, whenever
  I play it.

ten in texts, and however critics may deploy texts against 'bad' reders, do not the readers ultimately take their revenge on texts?

It will not do to put the question into a historical mode, and argue that whatever may be the case now there *once was* a Primary History that told the story down to that moment of annihilation of the people. For, on the one hand, it is rather difficult to prove that there ever was a Primary History as a single literary work that existed prior to the canonical collection of all the books that we have now (or something rather like it). And, on the other, if there ever were a Primary History it is not the Primary History as such that has survived, but the Primary History *accompanied by* the Secondary History. It is possible that some antiquarian enthusiasm might tempt us to support the pristine ideology of a reconstructed text against the bad company in which it now finds itself; but all we would then be saying would be that once upon a time there was a history of Israel that told its story as a tale of unrelieved gloom but that even in antiquity that history had been drastically qualified by being allowed to survive only in a context in which a totally different story provided the framework. The historical question, *Was* there ever a pessimistic history of Israel?, has an appeal limited to ancient historians; the literary question, *Is* there a pessimistic history of Israel within the Old Testament?, is of interest to every reader of the Old Testament.

The only answer to the question I feel able to give is that there *is* a Primary History, making a negative assessment of the history of Israel—if you are willing to see it in the Old Testament. The Old Testament contains the stuff for making such a history, and the marks of it are clear enough for many readers (though not all) to agree on seeing it. If you are willing to accept it, John the Baptist is Elijah who is to come (Mt. 11.14). But if you are not willing to accept it, he is not. John is not Elijah in the external objective world, not in any sense that will refute sceptics, but those who take him to be Elijah are under no misapprehension, and the implications they draw are powerful, intriguing, subversive, and creative.

Chapter 5

DECONSTRUCTING THE BOOK OF JOB*

At least since the time of Gregory the Great's 35 books of
Moralia in Job,[1] the book of Job has been regarded as a vast
quarry for moral truths and wise sayings about the human
condition. In particular it has been thought to offer the answer
to the knottiest questions about the meaning of life, the
problem of suffering, and the moral order of the universe. In
the bibliography of my recent commentary on chs. 1–20 of
Job[2] I have listed more than a thousand books and articles that
profess to state the unequivocal answers of the book of Job to
such questions. Can they all be right? If they cannot, is it
because their authors were incompetent, or might it be that
there is something about the book that lends itself to many
divergent interpretations? It is perhaps time, in fact, to wonder
whether the Book of Job, like many other works of literature,
if not indeed all, may be open to a deconstruction?

In this chapter I will be arguing that the book does indeed
deconstruct itself in several fundamental areas. I will try to
distinguish these deconstructions from simple incoherence,

---

* The first version of this Chapter was read as a paper in a sympo-
  sium on 'Narrative Strategies' at the Society of Biblical Literature's
  International Meeting in Jerusalem, August 18-20, 1986. The present version is a slight revision of the chapter with the same title in
  *The Bible and Rhetoric. Studies in Biblical Persuasion and Credibil-
  ity*, ed. Martin Warner (Warwick Studies in Philosophy and Literature; London: Routledge, 1990), pp. 65-80, and reprinted by permission of the publishers.
1 Gregory the Great, *Moralia in Job*, ed. M. Adriaen, 3 vols (Corpus
  Christianorum. Series Latina, 143, 143A, 143B; Turnhout: Brepols,
  1979-85). In English: *Morals on the Book of Job*, Oxford: H. Parker
  (1844-50).
2 David J.A. Clines, *Job 1–20* (WBC, 17; Waco, Texas: Word Books,
  1989).

and I will suggest that to some extent it is innoculated against its deconstructability by its rhetoric.

As a point of departure I take the well-known formulation by Jonathan Culler of the strategy of deconstruction:

> To deconstruct a discourse is to show how it undermines the philosophy it asserts, or the hierarchical oppositions on which it relies.[1]

Not every deconstructionist would be happy with such a transparent account of what in many hands is a very much more esoteric and mystifying procedure. Nor does this formulation lend itself to that aspect of deconstructionism that is a strategy in philosophy. But for deconstruction as a procedure with texts this is a statement which both seems understandable and sounds promising.

Some distinctions need to be made. To deconstruct a discourse is not simply to show its incoherence—which some writers have indeed attempted to do for the Book of Job, at least in its present form. For if a discourse should undermine the philosophy it asserts in the same manner and with the same degree of explicitness that it asserted it we should be merely confused or else amused at its incompetence as a discourse, and pronounce it simply incoherent. For a discourse to need deconstructing or to be susceptible to deconstruction the undermining has to be latent, as indeed the metaphor of undermining already tells us. In deconstructing, we are distinguishing between the surface and the hidden in the text, between shallow and deep readings. We are allowing that it is possible to read the text without seeing that it undermines itself, and we are claiming that the deconstructive reading is more sophisticated as a reading and at the same time more aware of the character of the text. It would therefore not be possible to challenge a particular deconstruction of a text by producing a non-deconstructionist reading; a deconstruction could only be called into question by arguing that those elements in the text that the critic thinks undermine it do not actually do so, and that the discourse is perfectly in harmony

---

1   Jonathan Culler, *On Deconstruction. Theory and Criticism after Structuralism* (London: Routledge & Kegan Paul, 1983), p. 86.

with itself throughout all the levels on which it can be read.

1. *Moral Retribution*

The first arena in which we may see the Book of Job deconstructing itself (or, we might prefer to say, in which it is open to deconstruction by the reader) is the issue of moral retribution, the doctrine that one is rewarded or punished in strict conformity with the moral quality of one's deeds. This is a view widely supported in the Hebrew Bible, above all by the Book of Proverbs, but no less by the theology of the Book of Deuteronomy or of the prophets. Pride goes before destruction and a haughty spirit before a fall (Prov. 16.18). In the path of righteousness is life, but the way of error leads to death (12.28). If Israel obeys the voice of Yahweh its God and is careful to do all his commandments, Yahweh its God will set it high above all the nations of the earth (Deut. 28.1). And if it is not careful to do all the words of the law, then Yahweh will bring upon it extraordinary afflictions, afflictions severe and lasting, and sicknesses grievous and lasting (28.58-59).

Now if we ask, What is the stance of the book on this central dogma of old Israelite religion?—which is to say in Culler's words, What is the philosophy this book asserts?—we are at first disposed to say the following. The plot of the book of Job affirms that in the case of Job the traditional dogma is false, for he is a righteous man who, to the surprise both of himself and his readers, suffers the fate of the wicked. On this reading, which is an ordinary reader's view as well as the scholarly consensus, the issue of the book is whether the conventional nexus between piety and prosperity, sin and suffering holds, and whether it is possible to make the usual causal inferences backwards, from prosperity back to piety and from suffering back to sin.

Given that this is the general impression we have of the book as a whole, we are bound to have some difficulty with its opening chapter, in which it is the very opposite that seems to be affirmed. For there the impression is definitely given, though it is not said in so many words, that the story of Job illustrates not the *falsity* but the *truth* of the traditional dogma. We first encounter what we suspect is the old dogma enshrined in the opening verses of the prologue:

> There was a man in the land of Uz ... blameless and upright,
> fearing God and turning away from evil. And there were
> born to him seven sons and three daughters, and his posses-
> sion was seven thousand sheep and three thousand camels
> ... (1.1-3).

The simple 'and', technically the waw-consecutive indicating
a subsequent action to that of the previous verb, is admittedly
all we have to go on. Nothing here says explicitly that we are
dealing with cause and effect, nothing prevents us from insisting that here there is a mere temporal progression or even
perhaps the laxness of a naive story that orders contempora-
neous facts into a temporal sequence to give the impression of
narrative—even though the only real temporality is in the
movement of the narrator's eye, first resting on this item, then
on that. Nevertheless, most readers find here more than mere
temporal succession; they notice at the very least, even if they
are not Hebraists, a sense of the fitness of things, an inner bond
between the piety of the man and his prosperity, between
rather his superlative piety and his superlative prosperity, a
fitness not only in kind but in degree, a fitness that is nothing
else, when expressed theologically, than the dogma of retribution.

So is this book in favour of the principle of retribution or
against it? Does it not look as if the book as a whole might be
undermining what it asserts in its opening lines on this
dogma? Suppose that we leave the question open for the
moment and read further down the chapter. Before very long
we come to realize that not only in the narrator's mind but in
the minds of the two characters, God and the Satan, the old
traditional causal nexus between piety and prosperity is evidently being taken for granted—in heaven no less than on
earth. Says God:

> Have you considered my servant Job, that there is none like
> him on the earth, a blameless and upright man, fearing God
> and turning away from evil? (1.8).

And the Satan replies:

> Does Job fear God for nothing, gratuitously? (1.9).

According to the Satan, God must be thinking that Job *does* fear him gratuitously, that the piety of Job therefore is un-motivated and is the origin of his prosperity. The Satan's own suspicion is that it is the other way around, and that it is Job's prosperity that is the origin of his piety, that it is only in order to become prosperous or remain prosperous that Job is so exceptionally pious. When the point is put to him, God has to admit that he does not know the difference; he had been assuming all along, as do most humans, that the principle of retribution runs from the deed to the result, and not from the result to the motivation. God therefore has to allow an experiment to be carried out on Job to discover whether the dogma of retribution, to which he has been giving his assent, is true. Now if the narrator of this book has God believing in the doc-trine of retribution, may we not suppose that the narrator was willing us also in these opening sentences to accept it, naively, yes, and unquestioningly, the way such dogmas are generally accepted?

This philosophy does not, of course, keep on being sustained throughout the prologue. For once the suffering of Job is determined upon a new world order has come into existence in which piety does not necessarily lead to prosperity and in which what it is that leads to suffering is not necessarily sin. In this second philosophy it is the righteous man who suffers. In the first philosophy only the wicked suffer.

Does then the first philosophy deconstruct the second, or, does the second deconstruct the former? Can we speak of either of them undermining the other?

No, not undermine. Just confront. There are conflicting philosophies here, indeed, but the warfare between them is all above board. For against the view that piety leads to prosperity the narrative affirms both the blamelessness of Job and the reality of his divinely imposed suffering. And against the cor-relative view that it is sin that leads to suffering the narrative affirms that, on the contrary, in Job's case it is piety that leads to suffering, indeed that exceptional piety leads to exceptional suffering. What happens in the narrative of the prologue is that the philosophy that is at first affirmed is then negated by the philosophy inherent in the events of the narrative as it unfolds. The first philosophy stands to the second as exposition stands to complication in a narrative; no narrative can get moving unless it begins to contradict the *status quo ante*, no philosophy is worth affirming unless in contradiction to that already affirmed or implied. That is all as it should be, and no more than we should expect of any narrative. There is therefore, I conclude, no deconstructing going on here, nothing that could be called an *undermining*.

Where then stands the philosophy asserted by the poem of 3.1–42.6, the core of the book as a whole? On the side of the first or the second philosophy? This seems open to no doubt. It is on the same side as the second philosophy of the prologue, that it is the righteous, not the wicked, who suffers; all it does is to expound it at length, dramatically and unarguably. What the poem does, philosophically speaking, is to prove over and over again that the doctrine of retribution is wrong. Every time Job's friends fail to carry us with them in their denunciations of Job, and every time Job excites our admiration for his injured innocence, the poem convinces us again that the doctrine of retribution is naive, dangerous, inhuman and, above all, false. If ever for a minute in the course of the dialogue we are tempted to believe that Job after all must deserve something of what he suffers, or if for a moment we find it hard to believe that anyone can possibly be so blameless as Job is making himself out to be, the affirmations of both the narrator and God in the prologue stride forward in our memory: there is none like him on earth.

Not that we are ever permitted to forget that the standpoint of the poem is, Athanasius-like, in opposition to the world that surrounds it. For the friends of Job, each in his individual way, begin all their thinking from the conviction that the traditional dogma is true, and Job himself makes no secret of the fact that he too, until these recent calamities, has always thought that way. He is the first to acknowledge that his sufferings are, *prima facie* at least, witnesses against him (16.8); he has always thought suffering was ammunition against humans, not testimony for them. It is this very break with convention, this brave shouldering of an unpopular commitment, that makes the philosophy of the Book of Job so universally recognized and treasured.

So far there has been the confrontation of philosophies, and the massive assertion of the second, that the doctrine of retribution is false. A surprise, however, is stored up for the last eleven verses of the book (42.7-17), of which it does seem to be true to say that they deconstruct the second philosophy in the direction of the first. Which is to say—since the second philosophy is the one affirmed by the great bulk of the book—the epilogue deconstructs the book as a whole.

The epilogue has often made readers uncomfortable. I suspect that the discomfort they have experienced has been the psychological registering of the deconstruction that was in progress. Until recently we did not have this name for the process, however, and so did not perhaps properly appreciate its character.

The discomfort is expressed sometimes in aesthetic terms, as if it were a lapse in literary taste to have the tortured Job first brought to a new religious and intellectual perception of the world—a vision that enables him to accept his suffering and bow before the author of it in reverence if not penitence—, and then to recount how on top of that he gets double his money back, for all the world like a contestant on some game show.[1]

At other times the discomfort takes the form of a historical judgment that the epilogue is to be assigned a secondary status in the history of the book's composition.[2] If we can affirm that it does not come from the hand of the master poet and thinker,

---

1 The nineteenth-century commentator R.A. Watson remarked (though he went on to reject this line of thought): 'Did Job need these multitudes of camels and sheep to supplement his new faith and his reconciliation to the Almighty will? Is there not something incongruous in the large award of temporal good, and even something unnecessary in the renewed honour among men?' (*The Book of Job* [ExpB; London: Hodder and Stoughton, 1892], p. 409).

2 'As an essential part of the old Folk-tale, [the Epilogue] could not be discarded. To have made the hero die in leprosy would have been too audacious a contradiction of what may have been a well-authenticated tradition' (J. Strahan, *The Book of Job interpreted* [Edinburgh: T. and T. Clark, 1913], p. 350). Similarly Marvin H. Pope, *Job* (AB, 15; Garden City, NY: Doubleday, 3rd edn, 1973), p. lxxxi.

the lack of fit between the poem and the epilogue can be lived with. In such a view there is, incidentally, a curious but commonly entertained assumption that to understand the *origin* of a discrepancy is somehow to *deal with* the discrepancy, to bring about a new state of affairs in which it is as if the discrepancy did not exist. It is, indeed, something of an oddity with this move in the case of the epilogue to Job that by most accounts the epilogue is not a chronologically secondary accretion to the poem, but the earlier folktale frame into which the poem has been slotted; so what is literarily secondary is not the work of some late and clumsy redactor (redactors being archetypically of limited intelligence) but pre-existent narrative stuff which the poet of Job simply did not excise. The discomfort is multiplied.

Yet another form the discomfort takes is a moral decision that the epilogue is not really very important. The story of Job, it is said, would be essentially the same without the epilogue. All that needs to be achieved by Job and for Job has taken place by 42.6, and the epilogue adds nothing to the poem religiously or philosophically. Job's restoration comes as a bonus to him and to those readers who require a happy ending, but it is really neither here nor there from the point of view of the meaning of the book.

Amid all this discomfort, it is even more disconcerting that what one hardly ever sees argued is the view that in fact the epilogue undermines the rest of the Book of Job. This is worse than uncomfortable, and that is perhaps why it is not argued. For who wants to argue that a world-class work of literature is so much at odds with itself as that, and so determined not to speak with a single voice; or, even worse, that a work of such great theological penetration ends up by giving assent to the very dogma it set out to annihilate?

For that is the position of the epilogue. It tells us, and not at all implicitly, that the most righteous man on earth is the most wealthy. If in ch. 1 he was the greatest of all the easterners, in ch. 42 he is simply one hundred per cent greater than that. And if there was any doubt in ch. 1 whether his piety was the cause of his prosperity and whether perhaps it was not the other way about, by ch. 42 no one, not even in heaven, is left in any doubt that it is the piety of Job, somewhat eccentrically expressed, to be sure, that has led to his ultimate superlative prosperity. What the book has been doing its best to demolish, the doctrine of retribution, is on its last page triumphantly affirmed.

Why not call this an incoherence? Should it be dignified with so glamorous a title as a deconstruction? Perhaps we can answer in the following way. In the switch from the first philosophy to the second in the prologue to the book we could see the familiar enough process of setting up a straw man that the rest of the book will demolish. But we are so unused to, or so uncomfortable with, the last page of a book pulling the rug from under all that has been going on throughout the book that we do our best to maintain that that is not what is happening at all. The very fact that the ending of the book of Job is not normally regarded as logically incoherent with what precedes it is an evidence that the contradiction which it embodies is no straightforward confrontation of philosophies but, in the strict sense, an *undermining*.

Should we not, however, before we throw up our hands in aporia and cry deconstruction, seek a *reconciliation* of the two philosophies? Could we perhaps argue that the central part of the Book of Job only sets out to show that the doctrine of retribution is not *inevitably* true, and that there can be notorious cases of its inapplicability? That the ending of the book wants to assert that despite the failure of the dogma to explain all human fortunes, in the end and in the main it is true enough after all? That even, perhaps, the case of Job is a special case, indeed an extraordinary case, maybe an utterly unique case? Has not the story itself been at pains to point out that this man Job is a man unlike other humans, that this man's fate is wholly to be explained by an unparalleled set of circumstances in heaven? So does that not mean that whatever may be true for Job is likely to be untrue for every other human? That the Book of Job, in the end, is not about Everyman, but entirely about the lone and remarkable individual Job?

If that is so, and that is where taking the ending 'seriously' (as they say) leads us to, then the poem has no philosophy to set forth, being about nothing at all except the unfortunate man Job. That would indeed be a short way with dissenting philosophies: simply showing that one of them is not a philosophy at all, and that there can therefore be no dissension.

No, perhaps that conclusion is too extreme. Let us take a different tack. Rather than assert that the Book of Job in its central section is only about the individual Job, and that Job is not typical of anyone at all, let us argue that it propounds the view that quite often the righteous suffer the fate that typically belongs to the wicked. Whether in the case of others it is heaven that is to blame or not hardly affects the issue. On this view, it is the *fact*, not the *origin*, of the suffering of the righteous that constitutes the philosophical problem of the poem. Then can we reconcile the epilogue of the book with such a philosophy? Could the epilogue be saying that if the righteous suffer, that is only a temporary setback? That the doctrine of retribution is to be applied to the broad sweep of things, and not to the trifling ups and downs of human fortunes? That, in such a case, what all the interlocutors should have been stressing was that Job, being by all accounts a perfectly innocent man who by cruel misfortune had been brought to calamity, could confidently expect that the dogma of retribution would come into its own in the long run and his end would be sure to be at least as good as his beginning? Very well; if that is what the book is saying, then the Book of Job is not about Job himself particularly, but about Job as a representative of a humanity that suffers what it does not deserve but is on the way to a happy dénouement. But such an explanation suffers from a problem of its own: if that is the philosophy of the book, how shall we accommodate the facts that Job is introduced to us at its beginning as an utterly exceptional human being and that his suffering is attributed to an unique event in the heavenly realm? How can the history of Job be representative of humanity? How can the unique be typical of the general?

These two quests for a reconciliation of the philosophies fail, I conclude. If, on the one hand, we attempt to house the anti-retributionist philosophy within the dogma of retribution, as a kind of modification or tempering of it, we denature the drama of the book. But equally, on the other, if we assert the retributionist philosophy of the epilogue over against the anti-retributionist stance of the poem, we rub the poem out of the book. That the poem should supervene upon the naivety of the prologue in its opening makes sense; but that the epilogue should undermine the grand poem and return us to the first naivety is disorientating, to the point of being deconstructive. What are we to make of a narrative that purports to conclude with a happy ever after but only returns us to the point where it all started, with what assurance that the same calamities cannot befall the doubly innocent Job? Is it so certain that lightning never strikes twice in the same place?

For a text to deconstruct itself means that there is no firm ground in it for the reader to take a stand on. Each time we begin to state the view the book takes of this fundamental question in theology and ethics—retribution—we find ourselves headed towards an aporia that is not merely a morass of indeterminacy in which it is difficult to discern what it is the book asserts but a truly deconstructive state of affairs where each of the philosophies it actually does assert is undermined by the other. Where that leaves us as readers is a point I want to return to at the end of this chapter.

2. *Suffering*

The second arena in which the Book of Job is deconstructible is its handling of the question of suffering. If we take as our starting point our general impression of the book (and why not? for that only means the preunderstanding we bring to it), we shall probably agree that a prime concern of the book is the problem of suffering.

What is the problem of suffering, in fact? Most of the textbooks on ethics and the commentaries on Job accept the commonsensical view that the problem of suffering is its *cause*, which is to say, Why suffering?, Why this particular suffering? And the book itself encourages us to regard that as its concern too; for it begins its narrative precisely with an account of how the suffering of the hero is decided upon in heaven—which is to say, with a narrative of a causal chain. Job himself of course has no idea of why he is suffering, but the book insists upon the readers knowing, and knowing in advance, and knowing all there is to be known about the matter. There is no question of any deferment of disclosure of real purposes or causes to the end of the story. Everything is up front; this is no story beguiling us with half-truths and false clues.

But the moment we ask, And what exactly was the reason for Job's suffering?, we run into a problem. The story bears retelling, if only for the soupçon of hermeneutical suspicion that can be introduced into the telling. What happens in heaven is that a question is raised that has apparently never before been asked, in general or in particular. The particular question is, Does Job fear God for nothing? The more general question is, Do humans fear God gratuitously? Job fears God, no doubt, but is it gratuitous, or is it for the sake of the reward? Heaven has been up till now as accepting as earth of the doctrine of retribution, which takes as its foundation the observation: the pious are the prosperous. But now the question is raised: Assuming there is a causal connection between the two, between piety and prosperity, in which direction does it operate? Could prosperity be, not the *result* of piety, but its *cause*?

The difficulty is that neither God nor the Satan knows which comes first, the chicken or the egg (or, as they say in Italian, as if to underline the problem, *l'uovo o la gallina*), the piety or the prosperity. This is no doubt because when the principle of retribution is functioning properly the pious are the same as the prosperous, and so you can never separate out cause and effect. We readers who have persevered to ch. 42 of course know by now what we think of the principle of retribution, but the God of ch. 1 has never engaged in deconstructions, dwelling as he does in an informal and somewhat rustic court, where there are none of the typical oriental courtesies but plenty of blunt speech, and no divine omniscience but only a willingness to find out, whether by report or experiment.

Experiment. That is the word. Job's suffering will be (not a wager, for the Satan has nothing to win, or lose, by the outcome, but) an experiment in causality. It is a simple matter to prove whether the piety hangs on the prosperity. Remove the prosperity and see if the piety falls. The experiment has to be done, not only for the sake of the truth, but even more for the sake of God's well-being. How could God ever look himself in the face if it were to turn out that none of his creatures, not even the most godfearing man of all, loves him for his own sake but only for what they can get out of him?

Which means to say that the reason for Job's suffering lies not in Job, not in the way the world works, or in the principle of retribution, or in any dogma, but deep in God and his need to know the truth about humankind and thus about himself (creators, like trees, have to be known by their fruit). Job suffers to prove God's integrity and to lay to rest the doubt the Satan has raised that perhaps no one in the wide world really reverences God for his own sake but that everyone is simply trying to use him.

Now the reason for Job's suffering is presumably not the reason for anyone else's. Once God has been convinced that gratuitous piety is possible, he does not need to experiment again to find that out. If none of the piety of this superabundantly pious man hangs upon his prosperity, the lesser piety of lesser mortals may also be equally clear of self-interest. Even if some people are pious for the sake of the blessings that will result, it is enough to have proved in principle that such is not necessarily the case. Job has answered the question of the causal connection between piety and prosperity paradigmatically and definitively.

Which then means: The reason for Job's suffering is never the reason for anyone else's. What the narrative gives with one hand it takes away with the other. For a moment we thought, when we were told the reason for Job's suffering, that we had penetrated to the book's explanation for human suffering in general. But that cannot be, for Job's case is unique. For a moment we were encouraged to believe that there is no mystery at all about suffering, that all is plain as day: Job suffers for a reason that can be simply told and which he could have understood as well as we can. But the instant we recognize that this reason is unique to Job, at that moment we are in the dark again about the meaning of human suffering generally.

So to the problem of suffering inasmuch as the problem is its *cause*, the book says, No problem. Here is the cause. But the moment we see it we realize that this answer is no good to us, for we wanted to know the reason for human suffering in general, and the book's answer has nothing to do with that.

How is it then that we thought in the first place that the book was about the *origins* of suffering? Is it because it purports to be telling us in its opening scenes about origins, causes? Not really, because it was claiming nothing, nothing more grand than to be a tale about an antique patriarchal figure from the days when wealth was measured in camels. But it succeeded in misleading most of the people most of the time. Can that be because it was really a deconstructive narrative, reaping where it did not sow, and more especially, sowing where it did not reap, sowing in our heads grand ideas of universal truths and never reaping but letting them run rank? Or is it deconstructive in the other direction, innocently maintaining it had no designs on the universe but all the time winning its way into world literature on the strength of its evident global human sympathies?

That deconstructive discomfort makes us wonder whether we should be trying another tack over this question of the problem of suffering. What will happen if we suggest that the real problem of suffering, for the book as much for ourselves, is not the problem, Why suffering?, but the problem, What must I do now that I am suffering?, or, How am I to suffer? That is, the existential question rather than the more intellectual question of origins.

On that route we encounter in the book first, not a deconstruction exactly but certainly a conflict. For the prologue makes plain that the response of a truly pious man to unexplained suffering is to bless the God who has given and who has taken away. The pious Job sees the hand of God in the predations of Sabaeans and Chaldaeans as much as in the fire from heaven and the whirlwind, and he accepts without demur that God has the same right to deliver 'evil' as he has to deliver 'good'. But the moment we turn the page into the poem in ch. 3 (by a happy accident, I have to do literally that in my edition of the Revised Standard Version), we strike against another image of Job, whose response to 'evil' is to abuse the author of it and demand he give an account of himself. It is a enormous shock to the system when we find God in ch. 42 approving of this rebellious and irreverent Job, and declaring that this Job has spoken of him 'what is right', unlike the friends who have spoken only orthodox theology in careful circumspection of God.

So although the book proffers two answers to the question, What kind of sufferer is approved of by God?, or, What should

I do when I am suffering?, it leaves us in little doubt about which is its preferred answer. It is not even a matter of its recommending pious acceptance so long as that is possible and the stiff upper lip does not quiver (in the mode of chs. 1–2), with approval being given to hysterical and venomous outbursts once they can be no longer restrained (in the mode of chs. 3–31). On the contrary, it appears to be the outbursts of chs. 3–31 that are being recommended. But that conflict of ideologies or behaviours is not one that leads in itself to a deconstruction, since the book resolves it, at least ostensibly, no matter how shocking the resolution may be.

Where deconstructive thoughts gain a toehold is over the issue (again) of whether the book speaks for humanity at large, or only of the isolated man Job. There seems little doubt over what was the right thing for Job to do, but does the book mean us to follow Job's example? We cannot help remembering that Job is the most pious man on earth, testified to by both the narrator and God (the former the more omniscient, but the latter presumably the more authoritative) as a blameless man. From the perspective of the narrative, he has a perfect right to protest against the treatment he is receiving, for he knows, and we all know, that he does not deserve it. But what of the rest of us? Does the book mean to suggest that protesting against one's suffering is a form of asserting one's innocence? Is it an indirect warning that no good will come of behaving like Job unless one is in Job's moral position to begin with? If that is so, we no longer know whether the book offers an encouragement or a warning. Is it saying, Behave like Job, or Don't dare behave like Job? What we are told about Job deconstructs the example he affords. Job becomes a example for no one, for is it not the case that 'there is none like him on earth'?

Thus, over the question of the meaning of the book in relation to the problem of suffering, we find ourselves forced into accepting by the logic of the narrative that Job's case can have no relevance to humanity at large, while every instinct we have about literature and life compels us in the opposite direction. It looks as though this Book of Job is another self-deconstructing artifact.

3. *After Deconstruction, What Then?*

When a text has been deconstructed, what happens next? This is a question not often raised by professional deconstructionists, who tend to believe in a never-ending spiral of deconstructions, but it is a pressing question for many other readers, who cannot bear too much dizziness and nausea.

One thing that happens is that the text goes on being read by readers who have never heard of deconstruction—and even being read pre-deconstructively by readers who have seen a deconstruction being performed before their very own eyes. Which is to say that the text goes on, to a greater or lesser extent, having the meanings it always has. A deconstruction does not mean that a text cancels itself out and becomes a mere cipher. Simple conflicts and incoherences may do that, but a deconstructed text loses little of its power in the deconstruction, though it may lose all of its authority as a trustworthy testimony to the way things really are in the external world.

What sustains a book's life beyond its deconstruction is its rhetoric, that is, its power to persuade beyond the bounds of pure reason, its ability to provoke its readers into willing its success even beyond its deserts. The Book of Job had already enjoyed a notable victory of rhetoric over logic long before the word deconstruction was ever breathed. For it had been persuading generations of readers to take sides with its hero Job in his ignorant reproaches against heaven even while they themselves have had perfect knowledge of what was hidden from Job. They have known that in heaven it is entirely accepted, even by the Satan, that Job is the most righteous of men, and they recognize that if Job knew that his tirades would be sapped of their energy. He would still, indeed, have something against heaven, for it still would be unreasonable of God to make an innocent man suffer in order to establish some theological point to the satisfaction of heavenly disputants; but Job would not be able to protest that his innocence was going unrecognized, and he would not be able to call God to account for branding him an evildoer. So he would be totally unable to speak many of his most moving speeches, for example:

> Be silent, let me alone! I must speak!
>   Let what may befall me.
> I will take my flesh in my teeth,
>   and put my life in my hand.
> He may slay me; I am without hope.
>   Yet I will defend my conduct to his face ...
>
> Grant me these two favours only, O God,
>   so that I need not hide myself from you.
> Withdraw your hand far from me,
>   and let not fear of you unnerve me.
> Then summon me, and I will answer;
>   or let me speak first, and you shall reply to me.
> How many iniquities and sins are laid to my charge?
>   Show me my offence and my sin.
> Why do you hide your face from me?
>   Why do you count me your enemy?
> Would you strike with dread a leaf driven by the wind?
>   Would you pursue a withered straw? (13.13-15, 20-25).

But we readers happily endure the contradictions of our position, privy to knowledge that undercuts Job's stance, and siding with Job nevertheless. Rhetoric triumphs over mere fact, and we would not have it otherwise. We are willing, as we listen to Job, to entertain the possibility that the prologue to the book does not exist and that there is no such perfectly simple explanation of Job's suffering as the prologue suggests. We recognize in the unenlightened Job the human condition, embattled against an unjust fate, and we will him to succeed in his struggle even at the moment when we know it is ill-conceived and unnecessary. Our assent to the logic of the story, in which Job will cravenly withdraw his charge against God the moment God chooses to communicate with the man, is wholly sincere, but we do not regret for an instant that Job has been kept in the dark so long; we were overjoyed that a man has had the opportunity, so properly seized and so long sustained, to approach his God 'like a prince' and 'give him an account of all [his] steps' (31.37). It did not matter in the least that all this defiance was, in a manner of speaking, the outcome of a huge misunderstanding.

In just the same way, no deconstruction can rob readers of what they have savoured in the Book of Job. Even when it has been deconstructed, the book can still go on exciting or entrancing us, enraging us against heaven or compelling our admiration for the divine, even assuring us that these and these are the truths about God and the universe. But when we believe its hero, we will believe him because we want to, because it suits our sense of the fitness of things, and not because he has divulged a truth about a transcendental signified that is one and incontrovertible.

The problem with the dogma of retribution or any other dogma is not that it is wrong, but that it is a dogma. And you can't cure the problem of a dogma with another dogma. Whenever you have a case of dogma eat dogma, you always have one dogma surviving and snapping at your heels. The heart craves dogma, even a dogma dying a death of a thousand qualifications. But the deconstructive strategy eliminates dogma as dogma, and in recognizing that multiple philosophies are being affirmed in the deconstructible text loosens our attachment to any one of them as dogma. It does not however follow that it weakens their persuasive force, their seductiveness. It may even be, sometimes, that when a fearsome dogma has been overpowered and shorn of its authority, we take to it more kindly and are attracted by its defencelessness, begin to find it charming, and even fall to wondering whether there was not perhaps some quality in it that might account for its having become a dogma in the first place.

Chapter 6

THE NEHEMIAH MEMOIR:
THE PERILS OF AUTOBIOGRAPHY*

> Everyone who wishes to be saved must become, as the
> Teacher has said, a judge of the books written to try us. For
> thus he spoke: 'Become experienced bankers'. Now the need
> of bankers arises from the circumstance that the spurious is
> mixed up with the genuine.
>
> *Clementine Homily* 18.20,
> speaking of a discriminating
> reading of the Old Testament[1]

> No such things as you say have been done, for you are invent-
> ing them out of your own mind.
>
> Nehemiah 6.8

The Memoir of Nehemiah may be argued to be the most
important historiographical source we have in the Old Testament. Unless we happen to belong to a quite small group of
scholars who doubt that the Nehemiah Memoir is the composition of Nehemiah himself, we shall probably accept that
there is no other historiographical document in the Old Testament that stands so close as the Nehemiah Memoir does to
the events it depicts. Where else in the Old Testament do we
find a text written within a decade of the events described,[2]

---

* A shorter version of this Chapter was read as a paper to the Chronicles, Ezra, Nehemiah Group of the Society of Biblical Literature at
  its Annual Meeting in Anaheim, California, on November 20, 1989.
  The theme of the session was 'The Nehemiah Memoir'.
1 Translation in *The Clementine Homilies. The Apostolical Constitutions*, ed. Alexander Roberts and James Donaldson (Ante-Nicene
  Christian Library, 17; Edinburgh: T. and T. Clark, 1870), p. 287.
2 Within a year or two only, in the case of most of it, says Williamson,
  distinguishing two editions of the Nehemiah Memoir (Hugh G.M.

events narrated by an eye-witness, and moreover, by the principal actor in the events themselves?

Admittedly, the Nehemiah Memoir is not exactly the book of Nehemiah as it stands, and our access to the Nehemiah Memoir is consequently second-hand and indirect. Nevertheless, even though the authentic text of Nehemiah's writing needs to be separated out from the larger Book of Nehemiah into which it has been edited, where else in the Old Testament, we may ask, is the work of the redaction critic so easy and its results so assured? Only the hyper-critical will disallow that in 1.1–7.7 (minus perhaps ch. 3), 12.31-43 and 13.4-31 at least we hear the *ipsissima vox* of Nehemiah.[1]

So confident may we be about the Nehemiah Memoir as a historical source that it would be possible to use it, one would imagine, as the foundation for a critical reconstruction not only of the whole history of Israel but also of the whole history of Israelite literature. Whatever the Nehemiah memoir knows of or presupposes, we could argue, must certainly be older than 430 BCE, and what it does not know or assume could automatically be placed under suspicion; for the Memoir is our one firm fixed point. From it we know, very well, for example, how things stood c. 430 BCE between Jews and Persians; we have a clear, though not very full, insight into Judaean society and the politics of the Jewish state; we learn about such diverse matters as prophets, arrangements for the Jewish cult, and the economics of Judaea. A systematic review of the Old Testament using the evidence of the Nehemiah Memoir as a touchstone for historicity would be, the more we think about, a highly desirable undertaking.

The only problem with basing anything on the Nehemiah Memoir is that Nehemiah is a liar. No more a liar, perhaps, than you or me; certainly no more of a liar than the average

---

Williamson, *Ezra, Nehemiah* [WBC, 16; Waco, Texas: Word Books, 1985], p. xxviii).

1 It is universally agreed, according to Williamson, that such parts of the book 'go back to a first-person account by Nehemiah himself (or someone writing under his immediate direction)' (p. xxiv). Similarly Joseph Blenkinsopp (*Ezra-Nehemiah. A Commentary* [OTL; London: SCM Press, 1989], pp. 47, 343-44), who however regards as inauthentic 1.1, 5-11a; 11.27-29, 33-36, 41-43.

politician of any place or time; but, for the purposes of historical reconstruction, a liar, who cannot be confidently believed
about *anything*. The difficulty with liars is that most of the
time they tell the truth; it is too tiring to be inventing lies all the
time. But their hearers or readers, once they have found them
out to be a liar in some particular, are usually incapable of
securely distinguishing the truth from the lies, and must, for
safety's sake, take *everything* they say with a pinch of salt.

If it seems at all shocking to call Nehemiah a liar, let us
rephrase that criticism in the more conventional language of
scholarship. What we will all agree is that in this apologia
Nehemiah is out to persuade his readers of his importance, his
selflessness, his energy—to say nothing of impressing his narratee, God, with his worthiness. And that desire will inevitably
have led him to highlight certain events, play down some and
distort others. This is what I mean by lying. Much of it may be
excusable, some of it may be trivial, but inasmuch as his story
does not correspond to historical reality (however we may
define that), and inasmuch as he is responsible for that
mismatch and is not just accidentally in error, his narrative is
a form of lying.

What makes it particularly troublesome in Nehemiah's
case is that he has chosen the first-person autobiographical
form for his narrative. The author has become a narrator, and
so has put himself in a position where he can deceive his readers into imagining that he, the historical Nehemiah, as author
has access to the privileges that narrators have—like insight
into the motives and intentions of their characters.[1]

---

1 Wayne C. Booth rightly pointed out that for most purposes the distinction between first-person and third-person narration is of little
consequence. But he made this important qualification: 'Choice of
the first person is sometimes unduly limiting; if the "I" has inade-
quate access to necessary information, the author may be led into
improbabilities' (*The Rhetoric of Fiction* [2nd edn; Chicago:
Chicago University Press, 1983], p. 150). It is precisely my point that
the first-person narrator of the Nehemiah Memoir finds himself in
difficulties which a third-person narrator might have comfortably
avoided. From the point of view of historical reconstruction, however, it is quite fortunate that we have the first-person narration,
because it draws our attention to historical implausibilities that
might otherwise have escaped us.

He is therefore an unreliable narrator. Now unreliable narrators, in my experience, come in two varieties: the overtly unreliable and the covertly unreliable. The covertly unreliable, like Nehemiah, are the worse. *Illywhacker*, a recent novel by the Australian Peter Carey, opens with the narrator's words, 'My name is Herbert Badgery. I am a hundred and thirty-nine years old'.[1] We, for our part, are not fooled. Even when Badgery goes on to tell us that he has always been a dreadful liar, but in the matter of his age he is for once telling the truth, and that he has documentation to prove it, we still know where we stand. If on the other hand he had told us at the beginning, covertly unreliably, that because he is sixty-six years old he is now retired and has a free bus pass, and then we had gone on to discover, somewhere about page 300, that he is really only forty-eight years old, we should have been *deceived* unless and until we had done the arithmetic. Ergo, covertly unreliable narrators are worse than overtly unreliable ones: they create more deception.

Suppose, further, the book narrated by this covertly unreliable sixty-six year old Herbert Badgery had been signed, Herbert Badgery, and the publishers had assured us on the dust-jacket that Herbert Badgery is a real person and the author of this book and not just its narrator, and had printed his photograph to convince us of the fact, we would have been in the position of most Biblical scholars working on Nehemiah. We would have been assuming that the author had been giving us a more or less reliable account of his life, errors and omissions excepted, when all the time there was buried in the book a time-bomb, a piece of information that the author *must have known was false when he wrote it*, but wrote it all the same. No one blames the authors of autobiographies for not remembering everything, or for misremembering things, or for being selective about what they tell of what they remember— though it might be argued that each of these things is a kind of lying; but if such authors distort reality, and we know they are doing it, and they know they are doing it, we are bound to have misgivings about using their work as a historical source.

1 Peter Carey, *Illywhacker* (London: Faber and Faber, 1985), p. 11. An illywhacker is in Australian slang a professional trickster.

How, incidentally, shall we handle the problem of *self*-deception? We cannot always distinguish between places where authors know what they are doing when they are deceiving us, and places where they are first deceiving themselves and therefore not aware that they are deceiving their readers. My solution is to say: identifying self-deception requires access to the mind of the author, which I do not have in the case of Nehemiah; so for all readerly purposes—which is what I am interested in here—I lump together the author's conscious and unconscious acts of deception, since from the reader's point of view they work the same way.[1]

There are four areas where I plan to probe the reliability of the narrator of the Nehemiah Memoir: narrative about his own mind, its intentions, feelings and motivations; narrative

---

1 Tamara C. Eskenazi's *In an Age of Prose. A Literary Approach to Ezra–Nehemiah* (SBLMS, 36; Atlanta: Scholars Press, 1988) contains an original treatment of the question of reliable and unreliable narration in these books. While affirming that in the Bible 'the omniscient narrator or implied author *for the book as a whole* is always reliable' (p. 132, my italics), she contrasts the point of view of the narrator of the books as a whole with that of the narrator of the Nehemiah Memoir, and implicitly makes the Nehemiah of the Memoir an unreliable narrator. She mentions three cases where 'Tension between the "I" of the memoirs and the third person perspective [of the overall narrator] occurs when Nehemiah claims credit for certain actions while the third person narrator speaks of how "they", presumably the community as a whole, accomplished the deed' (p. 134). I accept fully that this is an appropriate manner of establishing the unreliability of the narration of the Nehemiah Memoir, but in the present paper I am focusing not upon the disjunction between the Memoir itself and the narration which encompasses it, but on the internal evidence of the Memoir itself. It needs further to be noted that the reliability of Biblical narrators, recently re-affirmed by Meir Sternberg (*The Poetics of Biblical Narrative: Ideological Literature and the Drama of Reading* [Bloomington: Indiana University Press, 1985]) and Adele Berlin (*Poetics and Interpretation of Biblical Narrative* [Bible and Literature Series, 9; Sheffield: Almond, 1983]), is now being opened up to question. See, for example, David M. Gunn, 'Reading Right. Reliable and Omniscient Narrator, Omniscient God, and Foolproof Composition in the Hebrew Bible', in *The Bible in Three Dimensions. Essays in Celebration of Forty Years of Biblical Studies in the University of Sheffield* (JSOTSup, 87; Sheffield: JSOT Press, 1990), pp. 53-64.

about the minds of other characters, their intentions, feelings and motivations; matters of time, sequence, narrative compression, and reticence; and evidence of a romantic imagination at work.

1. *Narrative about the narrator's own mind, its intentions, feelings and motivations*

a. *Nehemiah's prayer (1.5-11)*

The first example I shall consider is not a very important case. It simply illustrates how easy it is to be taken in by the author as narrator.

When, at the beginning of his book, Nehemiah recounts how he heard that the walls of Jerusalem had recently been broken down, he prayed to the God of heaven. The words which he says he prayed (1.5-11) cannot of course be a *transcript* of his prayer. For, as narrator, he has just said that he was praying for 'many days', for three months, in fact,[1] and it is hard to believe that we are to suppose that he repeated this same prayer on each occasion. So already there is a literary stylization in operation: there are many actual prayers, probably with varying wordings, but only one literary prayer, which, if it was ever actually prayed, is unlikely to have been the prayer that was prayed on the many other occasions of his praying.

Nor is the literary prayer likely to be a *memory* of an actual prayer. For, we must ask, how long a time has intervened between the prayer of ch. 1 and the composition of the Nehemiah Memoir? It must be more than 12 years ago that Nehemiah has prayed this prayer, for in 5.14 the narrator tells us that he has been governor in Jerusalem for twelve years, and his actual prayer of course was uttered before he came to Jerusalem for the first time. After that space of time, can Nehemiah remember, for example, exactly which words of Moses he quoted in his actual prayer (1.8-9)?

The prayer is thus a *literary construction*, not a record or a

---

1 He hears the news in Chislev, the ninth month (1.1), but approaches the king only in Nisan, the first month of the next year (2.1).

reminiscence. If that fact is not obvious, there is one element in it that should make it plain. The prayer concludes with a plea to God to 'give success to thy servant *today*, and grant him mercy in the sight of *this man*' (1.11). The *today* is presumably the day on which Nehemiah will approach the king with his request, and *this man* is undoubtedly the king himself. But the king was not present when Nehemiah was praying any actual prayer,[1] despite what *this man* implies, and the prayer according to the narrator was the prayer of many days, not of one day, *today*, only. The prayer has been shaped literarily, most evidently at its end, in order to serve as a preface to the ensuing narrative of Nehemiah's conversation with the king in ch. 2.[2]

What has been happening is that the author has been behaving like a narrator. As an author he has access to events in which he was a participant, including events known to no outside witness—like what he said privately to God—and has put on the narrative the stamp of his own authority. It is ostensibly the truth because it is Nehemiah himself who tells us what was going on inside Nehemiah's head. But he has also been behaving like a typical narrator, shaping his material for his own narratival ends, and telling us lies (as narrators do) about the actual course of events in the interests of the narrative. If we were reading a Nehemiah Memoir written in the third person, and encountered a speech or a prayer put into the mouth of a character, we should not for a moment imagine that it had any authenticity, but would naturally read it as

---

1 It is another question whether he is present when Nehemiah prays the prayer of 2.4.

2 Williamson believes that the prayer is 'intended as a summary of the substance of Nehemiah's petition over several months and as such combines his general response to the news of v 3 and his particular prayer (v 11) when an opportunity to approach the king arose' (p. 168). This can only mean that it is a literary creation, even if it is close in spirit to the words Nehemiah actually uttered during those months. Williamson considers that the repetition of the prayer 'day and night'—which the prayer itself insists is actually the case (1.6)—need not mean that the specific petitions of v. 11 were repeated day and night (p. 173). If they are not, then 1.5-11 are not the words of any prayer, but the condensed report of many prayers *in the form of a prayer which was never uttered*!

a Thucydidean speech, the kind of thing the character should have said or might have said on the occasion. But when it is the author who is the narrator of his own speech, there is the possibility that he is telling us the truth, more or less, and it is not producing a sheer fiction. That leads some of us, in fact, to assume that he *is* telling the truth.

In the history of scholarship, the question of the authenticity of Nehemiah's prayer is indeed discussed, but the issue is invariably cast as the question whether the prayer whose text stands in 1.5-11 was composed by Nehemiah himself or by his editor, the Chronicler. Batten, for example, concluded that the prayer had no traces whatever of Nehemiah's hand, his memoirs elsewhere evidencing a 'peculiar, clear, succinct, and business-like style'.[1] Fensham, on the other hand, thinks that the Deuteronomistic language of the prayer indicates only that Nehemiah was well-versed in such phraseology, and concludes that 'there is nothing in this prayer that testifies against its authenticity'.[2] No one considers whether the prayer may be authentically by Nehemiah but a fiction nevertheless—which is what the internal evidence implies. Even Williamson, who thinks the language to be Nehemiah's but the prayer itself to be a 'summary of the substance of Nehemiah's petition over several months',[3] does not face the difficulty of the discrepancy between the historical actuality as he reconstructs it (many prayers with different wordings) and the claim of the text itself (one prayer composed on the day of hearing the news about Jerusalem, many times repeated).

If then our author on the first page of his narrative reports to us a speech he says he made on a specific occasion which he did not make, are we entitled to say, when we have established the unlikelihood of his assertion, that, nevertheless, something like what he claims actually did happen? Oesterley, for

---

1 Loring W. Batten, *The Books of Ezra and Nehemiah* (ICC; Edinburgh: T. & T. Clark, 1913), p. 188. For further discussion, see Ulrich Kellermann, *Nehemia. Quellen, Überlieferung und Geschichte* (BZAW, 102; Berlin: A. Töpelmann, 1967), p. 9 n. 16.
2 F. Charles Fensham, *The Books of Ezra and Nehemiah* (NICOT; Grand Rapids: Eerdmans, 1982), p. 154.
3 Williamson, p. 168.

example, argued that though the prayer of Nehemiah is no doubt an expansion by the compiler, 'the kernel of the narrative ... that he sought divine guidance as to what was to be done, is too natural to be doubted',[1] and Myers affirms that 'Nehemiah undoubtedly prayed on this occasion, particularly the kind of prayer given here'.[2]

Or are we to say, when we have found our author out in his fiction, that this is the kind of author we have, one who claims to be an eyewitness of and participant in the events he describes, but one who treats his material in the style of a narrator of fiction? Have we in the Book of Nehemiah one of the first examples of the literary genre of 'faction', 'fiction' written in the style of 'fact' ?

b. *The appointment of governors of Jerusalem (7.2)*
The point at issue here is again a small one, but it is a nice indication of the operation of the narrator's style. Once the wall of Jerusalem has been built, Nehemiah wants to make arrangements for the administration of the city. He writes.

> Now when the wall had been built and I had set up the doors,
> and the gatekeepers, the singers, and the Levites had been
> appointed, I gave my brother Hanani and Hananiah the gov-
> ernor of the castle charge over Jerusalem, for he was a more
> faithful and God-fearing man than many (7.2).

Readers think at first sight that they are being given reasons for the appointment of these persons: Hanani because he is Nehemiah's brother,[3] Hananiah because he is 'a more faithful and God-fearing man than most'. They then realize that Hananiah's being more faithful and God-fearing *than most* cannot truly be a reason for his being chosen. For if this were

---

1 W.O.E. Oesterley, *A History of Israel*, vol. 2 (Oxford: Clarendon Press, 1932), p. 120.
2 Jacob M. Myers, *Ezra, Nehemiah* (AB, 14; Garden City, NY: Doubleday, 1965), p. 96.
3 A case where simple nepotism probably served the interests of the state quite well. It goes too far to say that 'His own brother's loyalty was too well known to need chronicling', as T. Witton Davies does (*Ezra, Nehemiah and Esther* [CentB; Edinburgh: T.C. & E.C. Jack, 1909], p. 212); it is enough that Nehemiah's readers will accept the propriety and wisdom of keeping such appointments in the family.

the criterion for his appointment, he would have needed to be more faithful and God-fearing *than all others*, otherwise it is not being explained why he has been chosen. There is quite possibly nothing at all sinister here; it may simply be that the basic reason why Nehemiah chooses him is because he is already in charge of the 'fortress' (cf. 2.8)—but that is not what Nehemiah says. The narrator is pulling the wool over our eyes if he professes to be giving a reason (introduced by 'for') which turns out to be no reason at all.[1] No commentators, I observe, have found any difficulty with the wording of this sentence—which shows how susceptible they have been to Nehemiah as narrator![2]

c. Nehemiah's food allowance as governor (5.14-15)
The statement about Nehemiah's attitude to the regular food allowance due to the governor of a Persian province is an

---

1 Perhaps the Syriac saw the logical difficulty when it omitted to translate the last word of the sentence (מרבים) and put in its place the equivalent of Job 1.1 'and turned away from evil' (Wilhelm Rudolph, *Esra und Nehemia* [HAT, 20; Tübingen: J.C.B. Mohr, 1949], p. 138). Fensham (p. 210) thinks that the reason for giving this recommendation of Hananiah 'was probably that some doubt existed about his capabilities'; if that were the case, would this non-reason have sufficed, one wonders.

2 I leave aside entirely the question of whether the Hebrew text is correct here. It can be argued with good effect that the Hebrew originally referred to only one person, Hanani, Nehemiah's brother, and that Hananiah is nothing but a dittograph; so BHK, Sigmund Mowinckel (*Studien zu dem Buche Ezra-Nehemia* [Oslo: Universitetsforlaget, 1964], vol. 2, p. 29), Raymond A. Bowman ('Ezra and Nehemiah', in *The Interpreter's Bible*, ed. George A. Buttrick, [Nashville: Abingdon, 1954], vol 3, p. 724), L.H. Brockington (*Ezra, Nehemiah and Esther* [NCB; London: Nelson, 1969], p. 158), David J.A. Clines (*Ezra, Nehemiah, Esther* [NCB; London: Marshall, Morgan & Scott, 1984], p. 178), J. Gordon McConville (*Ezra, Nehemiah and Esther* [DSB; Edinburgh: St Andrew's Press, 1985], p. 112), Blenkinsopp (p. 275). The only difference this view makes to the comments above is that the non-reason for Hananiah's appointment would then apply to Hanani. Blenkinsopp thinks that the appointment of Hanani 'required justification in view of anticipated charges of nepotism' (p. 276)—which is somewhat speculative; the question remains, whether the reason given by Nehemiah would have satisfied.

interesting example of how Nehemiah the author, by intruding his point of view as narrator into the narrative, tries to have us think we have been given a satisfactory historical account. The text reads.

> The former governors who were before me laid heavy burdens upon the people, and took from them food and wine, besides forty shekels of silver. Even their servants lorded it over the people. But I did not do so, because of the fear of God ... I did not demand the food allowance of the governor, because the servitude was heavy upon this people (5.14-15, 18).

Almost universally, commentators accept Nehemiah's self-assessment uncritically.[1] The cost to his own finances of sustaining his entourage of 150 or more persons was, no doubt, enormous (5.18). But for him to claim that he refused to claim his entitlement from the provincial taxation because of the 'fear of God' is at best naive, and at worst a case of bad faith. What is this 'fear of God'? The implication of his claim is that any governors who cannot afford to pay these costs out of their own pocket lack Nehemiah's 'fear of God'; indeed, he explicitly maintains that previous governors—not excluding Sheshbazzar and Zerubbabel, we must presume—'laid heavy burdens upon the people', when all he can reasonably complain against them is that they collected what they were entitled to. What an unfortunate and unwelcome precedent Nehemiah is setting for later incumbents![2] It is fortunate for Nehemiah that he can afford to make populist gestures like reducing taxation, but it is irresponsible to let people think that it costs nothing to run a society or that the state provides no services that are of

---

1 E.g. Herbert E. Ryle, *The Books of Ezra and Nehemiah* (CamB; Cambridge: Cambridge University Press, 1893), p. 216: 'Nehemiah defends himself against a false supposition. His motive was not the desire for popularity with his countrymen; but the recognition of the Divine presence in all things quickened his sense of duty.' Ackroyd, by contrast, does indeed remark that 'We may allow here a little of that rhetoric by which a ruler contrasts himself to his own advantage with those who have preceded him, and so not look for too literal an interpretation' (Peter R. Ackroyd, *I & II Chronicles, Ezra, Nehemiah* [TBC; London: SCM Press, 1973], p. 285).
2 Clines, *Ezra, Nehemiah, Esther*, p. 172.

any value to them. Considering the personal esteem his action must have reaped for him, and the absence of grievances and conflicts over taxation he must have avoided thereby, it is hard to be taken in by his unqualified claim that his only motivation is 'the fear of God'. What is doubly disquieting, however, is a reflection upon how it comes about that Nehemiah has the personal wealth to support this troupe of retainers. He or his family have made their money either from trade or from land[1]—in either case from exploiting the capital or the labour of others. This is the way of the world, and there is no point in complaining about it. But let it not be said that giving with the right hand what one has taken with the left amounts to 'the fear of God'.[2] What, in any case, is Nehemiah to do with his enormous wealth now that he cannot lend it at interest (5.10)?

We here meet with, therefore, yet another place in the narrative where the historian finds it essential to distinguish between the narrator's self-portrait and the probabilities about the historical personage Nehemiah; it is another place where the narrator and his viewpoint deflects attention from the author and historical actuality.

2. *Narrative about the minds of other characters, their intentions, feelings and motivations*

It is a sign of omniscient narrators that they have access to the thoughts and feelings of their characters.[3] The narrators of novels do not need to explain to us how they come to know what people are thinking or what they say to one another in private. Nor do the authors of fictions of any kind. But when

---

1 It is all the more galling if, as Williamson has argued (p. 242), the wealth of Nehemiah and his family lay in estates in Judah itself.
2 We have no reason to question the religious motive which he adduces', says Blenkinsopp (p. 264), speaking for most. Is that very different from John Bright's assessment, 'By all the evidence, Nehemiah was a just and able governor' (*A History of Israel* [London: SCM Press, 3rd edn, 1981], p. 384)? Given that the evidence is entirely from Nehemiah, whether about his ability or his piety, is that very surprising? Should not the historian refuse to accept such claims at their face value?
3 See, e.g., Shimon Bar-Efrat, *Narrative Art in the Bible* (JSOTSup, 70; Bible and Literature, 17; Sheffield: JSOT Press, 1989), pp. 17-23.

authors writes as the first-person narrators of their work, we
are bound to ask how they come to know what they claim to
know.

In the case of the Book of Nehemiah, there are not a few
occasions when the author writes as if he were an omniscient
narrator. The effect is to persuade his readers, unless they are
on their guard, that what he says about his characters' feelings, thoughts and intentions is true, even though he himself,
the historical Nehemiah, can have had no access to the minds
of these personages. This technique works very well, for it
takes in most of the commentators and historians; they believe
that what Nehemiah says of Sanballat's intentions, for example, is true—for they have not been distinguishing systematically between what Nehemiah, as an author, can have known
and what he claims, as a narrator, to know.

a. *Sanballat's reaction to Nehemiah's arrival (2.10)*

The first example occurs when Nehemiah comes to the territory of Sanballat, that is, the province of Samaria (2.10).
'When Sanballat the Horonite and Tobiah the servant, the
Ammonite, heard this,' writes Nehemiah, 'it displeased them
greatly that some one had come to seek the welfare of the children of Israel.' Now it will have been a matter of observable
fact whether or not Sanballat welcomed him warmly or was
'displeased' about Nehemiah's arrival, but we need to note
nevertheless that we are far from having access to historical
reality in 2.10. For Sanballat may have been pretending to be
displeased, or Nehemiah may have misunderstood him, or
Nehemiah may have misremembered, or Nehemiah may be
lying. Whether Sanballat was pleased or not is something that
only Sanballat himself could tell us, and even so we would not
know whether we could believe him. One thing is certain:
Nehemiah is in no position to know the truth of the matter.

But it is more serious than that. When we consider
Nehemiah's remark that Sanballat and Tobiah were greatly
displeased that *someone had come to seek the welfare of the
children of Israel*, we are obviously in yet more speculative
territory. Can we imagine Sanballat using these words, or
anything like them? Can Sanballat have been such a racist, or
so blind to his own interests as a governor of a Persian

province, that the 'welfare' (טובה) of the citizens of a neighbouring province would have been so displeasing to him?
Further, would Sanballat have been thinking that what
Nehemiah was doing (building the walls of Jerusalem) was
'seeking the welfare of the Israelites'? Or is that not what
Nehemiah thinks he is doing, and is not the language entirely
from Nehemiah's point of view? And which was it, Sanballat
or Nehemiah, who thought of the inhabitants of Judah and
Jerusalem as the 'Israelites' (בני ישראל)? Would Sanballat himself not have called them the Judaeans? If then on so many
points the reasons for Sanballat's displeasure is cast in
Nehemiah's language, not Sanballat's, what reason remains
for us to believe in Sanballat's displeasure itself? Have we here
not simply Nehemiah's own point of view about his enemy,
and not a historical report?

It would not be a very serious matter what Nehemiah says
Sanballat believed were it not that most historians of the period
accept Nehemiah's claim. It is true that Ezr. 4.8-16 has given
evidence of Samarian hostility against Jerusalem. There we
find the Aramaic text of a letter purporting to be from an
official named Rehum in Samaria complaining to Artaxerxes
that Jews recently returned from Babylonia are rebuilding the
walls of Jerusalem, and alleging that the Jews' purpose in so
doing is to rebel against the Persian empire. The letter has to
be dated somewhere between 465 BCE, the year of Artaxerxes
I's accession, and 445, the year of the actual building of the
wall by Nehemiah. So that means that there is evidence that
some members of the Persian administration[1] in Samaria
within the 20 years prior to Nehemiah's arrival in Jerusalem
had had suspicions of the Jews. But for us to say on the basis of
that letter that the *motivation* of Sanballat—who was not
Rehum—was hostility to the Judaeans—which is what
Nehemiah claims—cannot be substantiated historically. Let
us grant that Nehemiah correctly represents Sanballat as

---

1 Whether Sanballat was the successor of Mithredath (Ezr. 4.7) and
  Rehum (4.8)—as Myers claims (Jacob M. Myers, *The World of the
  Restoration* [Englewood Cliffs, NJ: Prentice-Hall, 1968], p. 112)—or
  their superior is a question that does not need to be entered into
  here.

displeased; what conclusions are we entitled to draw about his motives? None. There are many possible motivations for Sanballat in this position: he might believe he has reason to suspect Jewish loyalty to the Persian throne; he might resent having a royal appointee with direct access to the king as his next-door neighbour; he might take an instant dislike to Nehemiah personally (and who could blame him?); or he could be simply mistaken about Jewish intentions. Does that make him hostile to the 'welfare of the children of Israel'? Indeed not. Narrators may read minds; but real-life persons, and authors, have to make do with guesswork. Nehemiah as narrator is hardly likely to be a reliable witness to the motives of people he regards as his enemies. But modern historians of the period are so good-natured that they prefer to take Nehemiah's guesses for truth unless there is evidence to the contrary. Is this a historical method?, I ask.

b. *Sanballat's taunting of the Jews (3.33-35 [EVV 4.1-3])*
Once the building of the wall has begun, the narrator tells us of Sanballat's reaction to the news of it:

> Now when Sanballat heard that we were rebuilding the wall, he was angry and greatly enraged, and he ridiculed the Jews. And he said in the presence of his brethren and of the army of Samaria, 'What are these feeble Jews doing? Will they restore things? Will they sacrifice? Will they finish up in a day? Will they revive the stones out of the heaps of rubbish, and burned ones at that?' Tobiah the Ammonite was by him, and he said, 'Yes, what they are building—if a fox goes up on it he will break down their stone wall!' (4.1-3).

A reader may well raise the question, How did Nehemiah know what Sanballat said in the presence of his 'brethren' and of the 'army of Samaria' (4.1-2)? If we accept Nehemiah's account of Sanballat's words and of his mood, 'angry and greatly enraged', we must be postulating either that Nehemiah had spies at the Samarian headquarters or in the army barracks, or that Sanballat and Tobiah conducted their conversation, in the presence of their fellow-officials and the army of Samaria, somewhere where Nehemiah could hear them, presumably just outside the walls of Jerusalem.

Do historians who reproduce Nehemiah's words as an

account of what actually transpired realize that they are making such a postulation? Batten is one of those commentators who read here a transcript of historical reality. He is correct in remarking that 'His words imply that Nehemiah had heard the jeering of the enemy'.[1] But he does not stop to consider whether Nehemiah is telling the truth; he simply assumes that he is, and adds, 'Doubtless Sanballat and Tobiah spoke in the presence of the people in order to weaken their hands'.[2] He does not, needless to say, give any thought to the circumstances that would have to be supposed for such a speaking in the presence of the Jerusalemites to be possible.

Would it not, however, be more probable to suppose that these are Nehemiah's words put into the mouth of Sanballat; that Nehemiah is, in short, inventing them? The subject will be raised again later, when we come to consider the prayer of Nehemiah interjected in 3.36-37 (EVV 4.4-5).

c. *Sanballat's plot against Jerusalem (4.7-8)*

Rather more important than whether Sanballat taunted the Jews of Jerusalem is the question whether Nehemiah's report of the planned military assault on Jerusalem by Sanballat had any reality, or whether it too may have been the product of Nehemiah's fertile imagination as narrator. According to 4.7—we should no doubt always be writing 'according to Nehemiah in 4.7', to point up the fact that the text has no validity beyond that of its character Nehemiah—when Sanballat and his supporters heard that the repairing of the walls of Jerusalem was progressing they were very angry (as they always are in this narrative), and plotted to march against Jerusalem and assault it, saying, 'They will not know or see till we come into the midst of them and kill them and stop the work'.

Among the questions we as historians are bound to ask is: How would Nehemiah know this? According to the RSV, some of Nehemiah's wall-builders, presumably those who lived in towns near Samarian territory, had kept saying to Nehemiah that 'from all the places where they live they [the Samarians]

1 Batten, p. 227.
2 Batten, p. 227.

will come up against us'. Alternatively, the Hebrew, which
seems to say, 'You must return to us', suggests that villagers,
frightened of the Samarians, kept sending emissaries to
Nehemiah pleading with him to send their menfolk back to
them.[1] But as historians we will recognize that rumour
among countryfolk does not really amount to evidence of the
actual intentions of Sanballat or of the existence of a military
decision for the deployment of the army of the Samarian
authorities. So how does Nehemiah know about the plan, or is
he just guessing?

If we cannot believe that Nehemiah himself had inside
information about the plans of the Samarian authorities, what
would count for us as evidence of a plan to assault Jerusalem?
We could gladly allow that a report of an actual attack on the
city would count, or even of the presence of Samarian troops
inside the territory of Judaea, or of Sanballat's soldiers mass-
ing about the walls of the city. But the text contains no such
word. Nehemiah says there was a plan to attack, which was
frustrated by God (4.15); since, from all he tells us, we gather
that there was in fact no attack, nor any observable signs of an
imminent attack, and he has not convinced us that he has any
way of knowing the intentions of the Samarians, historical
plausibility suggests that the threat was no more than his own
fear projected onto those he saw as his enemies.

Some historians have seen this point. Oesterley, for example, wrote:

> Whether more serious steps [than mockery] were taken to
> stop the building may be doubted. True, it is said in Neh. iv. 8
> (2 in Hebr.) that Sanballat and his followers 'conspired all of
> them together to come and fight against Jerusalem, and to
> cause confusion there' (cp. verse 11[5]); but nowhere is it said
> that any actual attack was made; moreover, it is difficult to
> believe that the governor of one province would attack the
> governor of another province who had the king's authority
> for what he was doing.[2]

And Miller and Hayes remark that 'the biblical text says
nothing about any actual enemy force being employed to

---

1 So Williamson, pp. 220-21, 226.
2 Oesterley, p. 124.

frustrate reconstruction'—forswearing any reference to what the 'biblical text' *does* actually say about an actual plot that was actually frustrated by Nehemiah's actions. More importantly, they note that the leaders of the neighbouring provinces were generally on good terms with the Judaeans (Neh. 6.17-19; 13.4-5, 23, 28)[1]—which casts some further doubt upon the plausibility of Nehemiah's account.

There are others who do not believe in the reality of a plot, but want in some way or another to save Nehemiah's reputation as a narrator. Thus Myers believes that there was no actual plot by Sanballat to attack Jerusalem, but rather a *rumour* put about by Sanballat that he and his henchmen would 'fall upon the builders by a surprise move and kill them'. 'When these rumours persisted (Neh 4.16) and alarmed the workers', writes Myers, 'Nehemiah was forced to take countermeasures.'[2] Myers neglects to mention that this is *not* what Nehemiah says; Nehemiah says there was a plot to attack, not a plot to spread a demoralizing rumour that they would attack.[3]

To much the same effect is the comment of Williamson that

> It is a moot point whether the alliance was in earnest in its stated aim of coming to 'fight against Jerusalem'.[4]

That is to say, we believe Nehemiah when he tells us there was a plot, but we doubt whether he was right to take it seriously. Why should we not equally doubt whether there was any such plot at all? What is the difference between a plot that is not

1 J. Maxwell Miller and John H. Hayes, *A History of Ancient Israel and Judah* (London: SCM Press, 1986), p. 470. It would be more accurate to say that *elsewhere in the Book of Nehemiah the author represents relations in this way*. Even this evidence does not amount to a transcript of historical reality; we are still shut up to the point of view of Nehemiah.
2 Myers, *The World of the Restoration*, p. 115. Similarly, in his *Ezra–Nehemiah*, he remarks that 'their bark was worse than their bite: they resorted to threats rather than to overt action since that would have involved them in difficulties with the imperial authorities' (p. 125).
3 Here is a familiar tactic of the 'biblical historian': faced with a biblical text one does not believe, one affirms one's unacknowledged modification of it rather than say one does not believe it.
4 Williamson, p. 225.

made 'in earnest' and one that does not exist? Was there a plot or was there not?

Others seem to be unimpressed by the Nehemian account, but curiously unforthcoming about what they think was the historical situation. Blenkinsopp, for example, having remarked on the presence of 'the traditional holy war pattern' in these verses, beginning with the notation of the conspiracy of enemies, restricts his comment to these very general words.

> The concerted effort on the part of neighboring provinces to frustrate the work being done with imperial authorization in Jerusalem gives us a glimpse into the problems faced by the central government in the more distant satrapies.[1]

Once more, readers find themselves asking, Was there a plot or was there not? Is the very notion of a plot just a creation of the author's to conform his narrative to the pattern of a holy war story? Or is a 'concerted effort' a plot by another name, and did 'frustrat[ing] the work' involve a planned military assault on Jerusalem? These are questions we need to know the answers to if we are to write the history of the period, and if we are to know how far we may accept Nehemiah's account.

Yet other scholars, and their number appears to be greater, take Nehemiah *au pied de la lettre*, even attempting in some cases to improve on his dramatic account. Thus, according to Bright, what happened is that

> When [mockery] had no effect, they incited—surely unofficially and while pretending ignorance of the whole thing—bands of Arabs, Ammonites and Philistines (ch. 4.7-12) to make raids on Judah. Jerusalem was harassed and outlying towns terrorized; according to Josephus (Ant. XI, V, 8) not a few Jews lost their lives.[2]

We note how the quotation from Josephus, who can hardly have had access to any source independent of Nehemiah's account, and is therefore *simply making up the deaths of Judaeans*, is used by the modern historian to reinforce the statement of Nehemiah. The historian would have us believe

1 Blenkinsopp, p. 248.
2 Bright, *A History of Israel*, p. 382.

that the plot was—to some extent at least—actually put into effect; for he writes: 'they incited bands of Arabs ... to make raids on Judah'. If that had been followed by the sentence, 'But nothing came of the incitement', the term 'incite' could have stood. But when it is followed by the words, 'Jerusalem was harassed ... terrorized', readers are bound to take 'incite' to mean 'incite effectively'—for which of course there is no evidence. It should perhaps be stated that the historian, even if he is right to accept Nehemiah's word that there was a plot by the Samarians against Jerusalem, is himself *making up* his claim that 'Jerusalem was harassed and outlying towns terrorized', since there is no actual evidence of such 'harassment'; he cannot be meaning to refer to mental harassment and terror alone, for the rest of his sentence about the loss of life makes clear that he is thinking of actual terrorist raids, even if he is not sure whether to believe Josephus about the loss of life.

Bright is not by any means the only one to take Nehemiah's account at face value. Even as sober a historian as Herrmann still reads it as historical reality.

> Sanballat ... made an alliance, sought to encircle Jerusalem and to launch a surprise attack on it. The plan failed. News reached Jerusalem in time.[1]

Similarly Noth had written:

> The governors of Samaria and Ammon gave orders for an attack on Jerusalem—no doubt unofficially, keeping themselves in the background—in which people from the south and west also took part. The plot did not remain secret, however. People living on the borders of the province brought the news to Jerusalem[2] so that Nehemiah was able to take defensive measures in time. When this became known, the attack which was intended to be a surprise, was called off.[3]

And Widengren to the same effect:

---

1 Siegfried Herrmann, *A History of Israel in Old Testament Times* (London: SCM Press, 1975), p. 312.
2 Noth does not remark that his interpretation rests entirely upon the LXX text, and does not in the least reflect the Hebrew (Martin Noth, *The History of Israel* [2nd edn; London: A. & C. Black, 1960], p. 324).
3 Noth, *The History of Israel*, p. 324.

> Sanballat and the others, however, when the walls were
> finished to half of their height, planned to attack Jerusalem
> in order to halt the undertaking. Nehemiah on the other
> hand acted with characteristic vigour and skill ... These
> measures deterred the opponents from an open attack.[1]

Serious historians, that is to say, put their signature to
Nehemiah's suspicion of a plot to make an armed assault
against Jerusalem, even though he gives no hint of how he
could have learned of such a plot, and the sheer possibility of
such an assault by one provincial governor upon another
seems rather slim. This is no way to write history, and it is all
due to Nehemiah's playing the omniscient narrator.

d. *Sanballat's invitation to a meeting at Ono (6.1-9)*

Here too Nehemiah as narrator claims insight into the minds
of his enemies. He knows that when Sanballat and Geshem
invite him to meet them in the plain of Ono that 'they intended
to do me harm' (6.2). And he knows that their general purpose
in the events recounted in ch. 6 is that 'they all wanted to
frighten us, thinking, "Their hands will drop from the work,
and it will not be done"' (6.9).

What is this 'harm' that Nehemiah believes they intend
him? If we turn to the commentaries, we find the following
fascinating variety of explanation.

> As Nehemiah knew, they had no other purpose than to do
> him harm.[2]

> Nehemiah hints that his foes plotted to assassinate him.[3]

> ... probably to assassinate him or have him assassinated.[4]

> Probably they wanted to make him a prisoner, perhaps even
> to assassinate him.[5]

1 Geo Widengren, 'The Persian Period', in *Israelite and Judean History*, ed. John H. Hayes and J. Maxwell Miller (OTL; London: SCM Press, 1977), pp. 489-538 (530).
2 Myers, *Ezra–Nehemiah*, p. 138.
3 Ryle, p. 220.
4 Witton Davies, p. 207.
5 Carl F. Keil, *The Books of Ezra, Nehemiah, and Esther* (tr. Sophie Taylor; Clark's Foreign Theological Library. Fourth Series, 38; Edinburgh: T. & T. Clark, 1873), p. 217.

They had to make fresh plans as to how to stop the work. The only possibility was to remove the person who had been responsible for the whole project. They decided to lure him to a place of their choice and to eliminate him ... Nehemiah suspected foul play.[1]

[W]e are not told what they contemplated: to capture him? or to assassinate him? to intimidate him? or to give opportunity for an armed attack on the city?[2]

[T]heir taunts and threats had not succeeded; they therefore changed their tactics and concentrated instead on eliminating Nehemiah himself from the scene.[3]

Nehemiah's enemies still tried to intimidate him by imputing to him rebellious intentions, or attempted to seize his person by cunning, in order to remove him (Neh. vi, 1-14).[4]

The character of the harm cannot be determined by the very general Hebrew word; but it is difficult to conceive of any other aim than personal violence, for the mere slackening of the work would be useless to these foes.[5]

Sanballat and Tobiah tried, on several occasions, to arrange a private meeting with Nehemiah, no doubt with plans to put him out of the way (Neh. 6.1-4).[6]

The failure of the enemy led them to make criminal plans. They attempted to capture Nehemiah (Neh. 6).[7]

Most of this, of course, goes far beyond what Nehemiah himself says. No one will seriously argue that in Hebrew 'to do harm' (עשׂה רעה) actually means 'to kill',[8] and it is something of a triumph for the narrator's art that he has persuaded so

---

1 Fensham, pp. 199-200.
2 Brockington, p. 154.
3 Williamson, p. 253.
4 Noth, *The History of Israel*, p. 324.
5 Batten, p. 251.
6 Widengren, p. 531.
7 Herrmann, p. 312. Curiously, Blenkinsopp sees in vv. 5-9, not in vv. 1-4, 'an attempt on Nehemiah's life' (p. 268).
8 Ryle, p. 220, followed by Witton Davies, p. 207 [read Esther viii. 3 for viii. 13], compared 1 Sam. 23.9 (of Saul) and Est. 8.3 (of Haman); though the contexts include killing, and killing is undoubtedly a form of 'harm, evil', this is nothing like evidence that the term *means* killing.

many critical thinkers, two and a half millennia on, to 'think
the worst' when all he used was an utterly general term![1] If
indeed Nehemiah had thought they intended to kill him, he
might surely have been expected to say so in as many words,
for he is clearly out to paint the most dramatic picture possible.
In fact, he makes perfectly clear to us what *he* believed their
intentions to be: it was that they wanted to frighten him into
abandoning the wall building (v. 9). How precisely he imagined they could do that is not clear, but obviously killing him
would not be a way of achieving that goal. We conclude that
the reconstruction of the intentions of Sanballat and his allies
by the consensus of modern scholarship is nothing more than
a fantasy they have copied from one another, aided and abet-
ted, no doubt, by the web of intrigue the narrator has so vividly
sketched.

That still leaves us with Nehemiah's beliefs and statements
about their intentions. Before we could accept his views, we
would need to assure ourselves of two matters: 1. Could
Nehemiah have had reasonable access to their intentions? 2.
Do subsequent actions of theirs bear out his suppositions (or
even, his information) about their intentions? On the first
point, only one scholar I have encountered seems to feel that
there is enough difficulty here for the matter to be worth discussing. Fensham writes.

> It is possible that he had received certain information which
> uncovered their plot; perhaps both sides made use of inform-
> ers. It is noteworthy that the enemies were well informed
> about the progress on the wall and Nehemiah was fully
> informed about their plans.[2]

Indeed, it is possible that Sanballat and the others had said,
Come, let us do Nehemiah harm (in general); and that some
spy of Nehemiah's had reported this to Nehemiah. But it does
not sound a very convincing piece of inside knowledge; it is too
unspecific. Is it not in fact rather difficult to plot to do harm in
general? Further, if indeed Nehemiah was informed about
their intentions, we should have to accept, for Fensham's

1 Blenkinsopp, p. 268: 'the offensive moved into high gear with an
  attempt on Nehemiah's life'.
2 Fensham, p. 200.

explanation to work, that they for their part were not informed that Nehemiah was informed about them; otherwise they would not have kept repeating the same invitation. It is indeed quite reasonable to suppose that the Samarians were well informed about the progress of work on the walls of Jerusalem, since that was always a publicly observable fact, but it is unreasonable to suppose that Nehemiah was informed about so private a matter as their intentions.

Secondly, do the subsequent actions of Sanballat and his allies bear out Nehemiah's suspicions of them? We are of course shut up to Nehemiah's account of their actions, and for the sake of the discussion we shall accept them at their face value. Sanballat does indeed challenge what Nehemiah is doing, and in that respect 'harms' Nehemiah. But harm is a relative matter, and it is perhaps arguable that Sanballat is not doing Nehemiah as much harm as Nehemiah is doing himself. In any case, nothing subsequently happens from Sanballat's side to threaten Nehemiah's person, and, as far as we know, the Samarians take no action whatsoever to sabotage Nehemiah's wall-building. It is true that Nehemiah believes that Shemaiah has been hired by Tobiah and Sanballat in order to inveigle Nehemiah into some cultic infringement 'so that they could give me an evil name, in order to taunt me' (6.13); but this is a far cry from a plot to assassinate the Judaean governor, and it does not square too well with Shemaiah's insistence that 'they [who are *they*?] are coming to kill you' (6.10).

What are Sanballat's intentions, in fact, at least as we can infer from them from what Nehemiah reports to us Sanballat actually says? Sanballat's letter reports a rumour that is circulating in various provinces, that the significance of the wall-building is that the Jews intend to rebel against the Persian empire, and that Nehemiah intends to become the king of the Jews. Sanballat observes that this rumour will be reported to the king, and therefore invites Nehemiah to come and discuss the matter (6.6-7).

These are of course very serious allegations, and they have a certain plausibility. We note, however, that Sanballat does not say that they are his views, but that it is a general rumour; he does not say that he intends to report it to the king, but that the king is bound to hear it. He does not call upon Nehemiah to issue a denial or to stop the wall-building, or anything other than to come to discuss the matter. If Nehemiah knows something more concrete about Sanballat, something that he is not telling us, then we have no further chance of historical reconstruction; but if he is inferring Sanballat's hostility to him from this letter in itself, is he not jumping to conclusions?

Everyone remarks on how unscrupulous Sanballat is in including the gossip about Nehemiah's plans for rebellion in an *open letter*! That is indeed what Nehemiah would have us think.[1] But no one remarks on the significance of the fact—a fact by Nehemiah's own admission—that Sanballat has sent the news of the rumour to Nehemiah four times already *as a sealed letter* (6.5). Is that the action of a mere trouble-maker? Is there not more to Sanballat's action than Nehemiah would have us believe? We have nothing further to go upon, and we cannot reconstruct Sanballat's intentions; but Nehemiah's narration does not satisfy our reasonable questions; rather it prompts them.

There is more to worry us in this account. A reliable narrator would justify Nehemiah's suspicions about Sanballat and his intentions by the terms in which he had Nehemiah reply. An unreliable narrator finds no necessity to make one part of his story cohere with another—to make, for example, Nehemiah's reading of Sanballat's intentions match with Nehemiah's riposte to Sanballat's invitation. He allows us, indeed, to start thinking: if these are the terms in which Nehemiah replies to Sanballat, he cannot have been very worried about the threat he says he suspected when he received the letters. For, first, on the matter of the wall-building, Nehemiah has in his possession authorization for it from the king, including requisition orders for the materials required. So why does he simply deny the accusation? Why does he not fall back on his official commission to support him?

---

1 Cf. Clines, *Ezra, Nehemiah, Esther*, p. 174: 'Sanballat, in a classic example of gamesmanship, writes a letter which professes concern for Nehemiah but which passes on a piece of gossip to the effect that Nehemiah is plotting rebellion against the empire; and he sends it as an open letter!'

And on the matter of his supposed ambition to become king, why does he not affirm his loyalty to the Persian king, allow that his ambition is indeed to be the leader of the Jews (whatever the designation for that office may be), but point out that he cannot, no matter how hard he tries, become king because he is not a Davidide?[1] Why does he make the feeble reply that 'No such things as you say have been done, for you are inventing them out of your own mind'? (6.8). This is the standard blanket denial of a politician—which no one believes and most take as an implicit confession. Worse still, such an unreasoned denial is going to do Nehemiah no good at all with the king when the rumour does reach him. Of course Nehemiah denies he is planning rebellion. So does every rebel. Which coup d'état was announced the week before in the newspapers? If Nehemiah truly does not want the charge to stick, he has to offer some account of himself that will show how unreasonable it is. Is there not something deeply implausible about the narrative here? Can we accept *both* that there there was a serious charge against Nehemiah's loyalty *and* that he treated it with such sangfroid? Or is the narrator having us on, in some respect or another?

There is something odd, too, about Nehemiah's form of words, 'no such thing has been done' (לא נהיה כדברים האלה, 6.8). For the gravamen of the allegation against him is not about things that *have been done* but things that are being *intended* (to rebel, to become king). Of the two things that are said in the allegation to *have been done*, one in fact *has* been done (building the wall), and there can be no dispute about that, while the other, which presumably has not been done, is the setting up of prophets. Why does Nehemiah deny only that item? And what is a denial worth that he has himself *not set up prophets to proclaim him king*, when it is really immaterial whether the alleged prophets have been instigated by him or merely tolerated by him. What any Persian official, or monarch, would want to know is whether or not there were indeed prophets—or anyone at all, for that matter—walking

---

1 Of course, there have been scholars who have believed he was; see especially Kellermann, pp. 157-58. For the opposite opinion, which is more widely held, see, e.g., Blenkinsopp, p. 269.

about in Jerusalem urging Nehemiah's claims as pretender to the Jewish throne. The question, Under whose auspices are they operating?, would be a mere technicality and entirely beside the point. We readers are intrigued to learn that Nehemiah does not for a moment deny there are such prophets, but merely that he has not set them up.

The long and short of it is that Nehemiah as author does not offer a satisfactory response to the allegations, and does his cause no good by his cavalier response to Sanballat. He has persuaded himself, for it is he after all who narrates his reply, that such a reply is all that Sanballat deserves; but if he is telling us the truth about Sanballat's allegations, it is Nehemiah who has done himself the most harm in this situation. It is not only Nehemiah the character who is giving a hostage to fortune by failing utterly to scotch the rumour about himself. It is also Nehemiah the narrator who sows deep suspicions in his readers' minds about the truth and coherence of his narrative.

Before leaving this episode, we should review Ackroyd's suggestions on the matter, and Williamson's response. On 6.2 Ackroyd comments that

> it is possible that [Nehemiah's] suspicions were over-easily aroused and that there was at least some concern for a discussion aimed at easing tension. The other governors in the area could not afford to lose favour with Persian authority ... [W]e may perhaps see that there is another side to the case, and remind ourselves that we are reading this account entirely from the viewpoint of Nehemiah.[1]

To these remarks Williamson has replied that, 1. if Sanballat's motive had been genuine concern, he could have offered to come to Jerusalem himself; 2. neither his attitude before (3.33-35 [EVV 4.1-3]) nor after (6.5-9) the invitation to Ono looks like that of someone attempting reconciliation; 3. from Sanballat's point of view, Nehemiah himself must have been the real obstacle to friendly relations between Samaria and Jerusalem, and the obvious solution was the elimination of Nehemiah.[2]

As for the first point, it can easily be agreed that little success

1 Ackroyd, pp. 286-87.
2 Williamson, p. 254.

in historical reconstruction is likely to come from attempts to whitewash the personages of the narrative. We do not have to accept that Sanballat's motive was 'genuine concern' for Nehemiah. He may well have been fearful, as Nehemiah's next-door neighbour, for his own political position and he may well have entertained not the slightest affection for Nehemiah. The question is, however, not whether Sanballat had genuine concern for Nehemiah but whether Sanballat's interest was the 'elimination' of Nehemiah. It it were, it is surprising that his only tactic was to attempt to inveigle Nehemiah away from Jerusalem, especially when that proved spectacularly unsuccessful. And even if, subsequently, he stood behind Shemaiah's attempt to frighten Nehemiah into hiding in the temple, that does not seem the ploy of a man intent upon 'eliminating' his opponent.

Secondly, it is not necessary to suppose that Sanballat's concern is *either* 'reconciliation' with Nehemiah *or* 'elimination' of him. It would make perfectly good sense, if Sanballat is fearful that Nehemiah's fortification of Jerusalem will have unfortunate repercussions on other provinces in the region as well, that he should be proposing to discuss with him some means of damage-limitation.

Thirdly, even if it is correct that Sanballat regarded Nehemiah as himself the chief stumbling block to relations with Jerusalem, it does not follow that the only step Sanballat could have envisaged was the 'elimination' of Nehemiah. There must be many ways of neutralizing a political opponent short of assassination.[1]

Williamson further remarks, à propos of Sanballat's open letter, that

> Sanballat seems to have overlooked the.considerations (i) that a secret meeting with Nehemiah in such circumstances might itself be construed as collaboration in rebellion, and (ii) that to seek a secret consultation after sending an open letter was somewhat self-contradictory.[2]

These are very reasonable observations, but we can surely

---

1 Nehemiah himself believed he had identified one such attempt in the bribing, as he thought it, of Shemaiah (6.12-13).
2 Williamson, p. 257.

reply that it is improbable that the governor of a Persian province can have been so naive; and that therefore, some revision of our understanding of the historical actuality is in order, especially when the only evidence we have of Sanballat's intentions and actions is the narrative of a hostile witness.

No doubt there is no way of our knowing exactly what Sanballat's intentions were, and all we can do is to register our dissatisfaction with the account of them given by Nehemiah as being unconvincing and incoherent. Modern historians cannot afford to let themselves be taken in by Nehemiah the narrator, but must always check the claims of the narrator against what they can reasonably believe about the historical personage Nehemiah.

3. *Time, Sequence, Narrative Compression, and Reticence*

While life itself is lived in chronological sequence, and while history 'as it actually happened' is nothing but 'one damn thing after another', narrators habitually play ducks and drakes with chronology. There is nothing reprehensible about this; it is, no doubt, the only way of making a story out of anything or finding significance in the intrinsically meaningless flux of events. Narrators consequently compress events, skip, and otherwise disorder the course of their history; they go in for flashbacks, anticipations, and suchlike dischronologizations.

The historian, on the other hand, has as a first task the reconstruction of the actual sequence of events so far as is possible, since all the interesting things that can be said about causes and results, about circumstances and factors, about movements and trends, rest entirely upon knowing what preceded what. When historians make use of literary works, then, they have to disentangle an actual sequence of events from the narrator's created order. In the case of the Book of Nehemiah, they have very often overlooked the fact that it is a literary construction and have tried to use it as if it were a chronicle giving first-hand access to historical actuality. The reason why historians' usual critical abilities seem to fail them in this particular enterprise seems to be that they have attuned themselves to Nehemiah as author, and have forgotten that the Nehemiah we meet with in the book is in the first place a narrator.

a. *Sanballat's conversation with Tobiah and Nehemiah's prayer (3.33-38 [EVV 4.1-5])*
As at several points in his narrative, the narrator breaks frame at 3.36-37 (EVV 4.4-5), becomes for the moment an 'overt narrator',[1] and addresses a prayer in his own voice to God. This does not purport to be the report of a prayer uttered by the character Nehemiah at the moment the narrative has just reached, for there is no introductory phrase locating it as a speech of the character.[2] We could, of course, easily imagine what such a phrase might be, on the basis of 2.5 'And I prayed to the God of heaven'. It must then be an interjection by the narrator at this point in the narrating; and since the narrating is to be understood as taking place at the moment of composition of the Nehemiah Memoir, the prayer of Nehemiah must also be understood as the prayer of the author Nehemiah uttered by the author at the time he is writing—which is to say, some time after the 32nd year of Artaxerxes (cf. 5.14), or 12 years at least after the time that is being described in the narrative.

Nevertheless, and this is where the narration is misleading, it is evident that the words of the prayer represent not the situation of the *composing* of the narrative but the situation of the events told in the narrative; they represent the stance of the character Nehemiah at this moment in the narration, not the stance of the narrator. Three elements in the prayer make this plain. First, God is called on to 'hear'. This language is in fact quite problematic, but I can nevertheless find no commentator who thinks it so, and who considers what it could be that God is called on to hear. God cannot be invoked to 'hear' the

---

1 For the terminology, cf. Bar-Efrat, *Narrative Art in the Bible*, pp. 23-32.

2 GNB finds it necessary to preface vv. 4-5 with 'I prayed'—but that of course is not there, and to add it spoils the point. Fensham says, 'When he heard about the scorn of the enemies and especially their ridicule heaped on the builders, Nehemiah prayed to God' (p. 181; similarly Keil, p. 201); but he does not remark on the absence of any phrase linking the prayer with the narrated situation.

words that the author Nehemiah is at this moment engaged in writing, for he cannot *hear* words that are *written*. And he cannot 'hear' words that were spoken more than 12 years ago. He can only hear *spoken* words, words that are *just now* being spoken. That is, the setting of the prayer must be the situation of the taunting. Secondly, Nehemiah says that 'we are despised'. Now, no doubt the Jews were despised by various persons at various times, but the moment of despising that evokes this prayer of Nehemiah's is unquestionably the moment of the speeches of Sanballat and Tobiah. It is their 'mockery' (לעג, 3.33 [4.1]) that constitutes the 'despising' (בוזה) and 'reproach' (חרפה, 3.36 [4.4]) of which Nehemiah complains. Thirdly, the 'provocation' by Sanballat has taken place 'before the builders';[1] since there are no builders around at the time of the composition of the narrative, but only ex-builders, the wall-construction having been completed some twelve years previously, the term 'builders' pinpoints the point of view of the prayer, chronologically speaking, as the time of the taunting. The only commentator to have taken proper cognizance of these facts is Kidner, who writes:

> This sudden prayer ... transports the reader back to the very moment of dismay, as if this were an extract from the day's record, simply copied as it stood. Even if it is a more distant recollection, Nehemiah is immersed again in the experience as he writes.[2]

There is, of course, little likelihood that there was a 'day's record' in which Nehemiah, like a modern-day cabinet minister, recorded his recollections of the day's activities in order to use them at a later date to justify himself and put his opponents in the wrong. But that is indeed the impression the text gives us, or alternatively, as Kidner puts it, that Nehemiah is immersed again in the experience. But the prayer is composed

---

1 I leave aside here the question of whether the object of כעס, 'provoke', is God (understood) or the builders themselves; for a recent discussion, see Williamson, p. 214.

2 Derek Kidner, *Genesis. An Introduction and Commentary* (TOTC; London: Tyndale Press, 1967), p. 91. Williamson is no doubt thinking similarly when he writes that the interjected prayers in the Nehemiah Memoir 'add a vivid contemporaneity to the account', but the point is not developed.

and narrated in hindsight, at the time of the narrating, not at the time when the event is supposed to have occurred.

So the prayer of Nehemiah is not what it purports to be; there is a large contamination of the narrative of the past by the present act of narrating, and a confusion of the person of Nehemiah with the narrator Nehemiah. There is nothing improper about that; in fact it is quite an effective dramatic device for transporting the reader to the time of the events depicted, as Kidner says. But what follows is that this prayer cannot be used as a historical source for reconstructing the circumstances of the taunts of Sanballat and Tobiah. It is nothing but a *literary construction*.

Nonetheless, some scholars do use it as a historical source, surprisingly enough. Williamson, for example, who is more than most alert to the literary aspect of the narrative, finds in the phrase 'before the builders'

> the first indication we have that this whole scene has been played out within earshot of the builders. By withholding this information until now, Nehemiah certainly gives it maximum dramatic impact: the exchanges are not behind the isolation of closed doors but at a point of close psychological encounter.[1]

But what is implied in these remarks for the reconstruction of the historical actuality? Williamson does not go so far as to tell us where Sanballat and Tobiah may be supposed to be standing when they uttered these remarks 'within earshot of the builders'; but it would surely be important for our understanding of the events if we knew that on some occasion Sanballat and Tobiah and the army of Samaria[2]Alt, A. and his allies (?

---

1 Williamson, p. 217. Cf. p. 216, where he says that Sanballat's 'scorn is voiced, not merely in the hearing of the wall-builders, but in the presence of his allies'.

2 What is this 'army of Samaria', by the way? Myers remarks (p. 123) that Samaria was not a military colony, and falls back on Alt's suggestion that the term refers to the *'am ha'arets*, the officials and important citizens around him (Albrecht Alt, 'Die Rolle Samarias bei der Entstehung des Judentums', in *Festschrift Otto Procksch zum 60. Geburtstag* [Leipzig: A. Deichert und J.C Hinrichs, 1934], pp. 5-28 (13) (= his *Kleine Schriften zur Geschichte des Volkes Israel* [München: C.H. Beck, 1953], vol. 2, pp. 316-37 [323]); simi-

the Arabs and Ammonites and Ashdodites of 4.1 [EVV 4.7])
stood within earshot of the wall-builders and taunted them.
Blenkinsopp indeed believes that the last words of the prayer

> suggest that the disparaging remarks of Sanballat and
> Tobiah were meant to be heard by the builders ... If so, the
> incident must have occurred just outside Jerusalem rather
> than in Samaria, a circumstance which would heighten the
> element of danger and explain the allusion to the military
> escort.[1]

If that were indeed the case, would the narrative of 3.33-37
(EVV 4.1-5)—in which there is no reference to all these people
travelling to Jerusalem, nor to any effect of this show of force
upon the Jerusalemites, but rather the statement that these
words were spoken 'in the presence of his brethren and of the
army of Samaria'—be a natural way of giving us this information? How far outside Jerusalem do you have to stand for
your words to be heard? Or is it not rather the case that the
whole idea of a visit to Jerusalem by Sanballat and his cronies
rests upon a misunderstanding of the genre of Nehemiah's
prayer, and a confusion of the narrator with the author?

b. *Nehemiah's interview with the king (2.1-8)*
There are many oddities about this conversation, but perhaps
the greatest oddity is the way in which commentators seem to

larly Rudolph, p. 121. Witton Davies guessed it was 'a body of
"irregulars" belonging to Samaria and the parts around, sworn to
defend the Persian authority in all emergencies' (p. 191); this is a
complete fabrication, of course. Williamson relies on Ezr. 4.23,
'Rehum and Shimshai went in haste to the Jews at Jerusalem and
by force and power made them cease', to prove that 'it is certain
that the governor of Samaria had some troops under his command'
(p. 216). But we must ask, Is the use of troops the only possible way
of using 'force and power', what evidence do we have that the Aramaic chronicle editor of 4.23 knew anything about troop arrangements in Samaria, and are we to suppose that Nehemiah too, as a
Persian governor, had troops at his disposal? Or did he have to rely
on his own personal bodyguard of 'lads' (נערים)? Are the 'overseers'
(פקיד) of Neh. 11.9, 14 and the 'mighty men of valour' of 11.14 military personnel (as Clines, pp. 215-16)? There are many questions to
be asked before we can feel confident that we are dealing with historical reality here.

1 Blenkinsopp, p. 245.

take it for granted that the narrative is a tape-recording of some actual conversation. If this had been a third-person narration, and the author had not been Nehemiah himself, no one would have doubted that the conversation was fictional; but it seems to be impossible for most scholars to imagine Nehemiah writing a fiction about himself, even though they gladly acknowledge that the book as a whole is an apologia for its author, presenting him at each point in the most favourable light. Nor does anyone take into consideration that, even if the conversation actually took place, there is a gap of at least twelve years between the event and the narrating of it; and no matter how important such a conversation would have been in the life of Nehemiah, there will have been plenty of opportunity for misremembering and distortion to have played a part over those years.

One way in which the confusion of narrator and author operates for the reader is a writerly habit of commentators. They persistently use the historic past tense to recount narrated events. When they write, for example, that 'Nehemiah explained the reason for his dejection', 'the king understood at once the point of Nehemiah's complaint', 'Nehemiah was therefore naturally apprehensive',[1] the reader has no way of knowing whether they believe that such was in fact the case or whether they are simply reporting the narrative and elaborating it from its own narratorial point of view. Since this is just the way commentators would be writing if they really believed that the narrative was an accurate transcript of events, the reader may be forgiven for doubting whether they are making any real distinction between historical actuality and the narrative.

This issue comes to the fore at several points. The only one I shall discuss here is the matter of whether Nehemiah was appointed governor of Judaea while he was still at the Persian court. According to the narrative of ch. 2, he is sent to Jerusalem to rebuild the city, and nothing is said of any appointment to the governorship; according to 5.14, however, his appointment as governor of the province of Judaea runs

1 The quotations come from Blenkinsopp, p. 214, but such language could have equally well been cited from almost any commentator.

from that same year of Artaxerxes in which he was given permission to go to Jerusalem. If we are at all concerned with plausible historical reconstruction, it is hard to believe that Nehemiah's commission was to any other office than that of governor from the first, for the following reasons: 1. It is difficult to suppose that there was any governor of Judaea in office at the time of Nehemiah's commission, whom Nehemiah shortly supplanted but said nothing of it.[1] 2. Nehemiah was, so far as we know, the only royal appointee within the province. 3. The execution of his project would have required not only the provision of materials, which is mentioned in ch. 2, but also major authority for finance and manpower—which would have put him in an impossible conflict with a governor, if there was one. 4. The rebuilding of Jerusalem cannot have been viewed in the Persian court as a matter of sentiment but as a delicate political and strategic operation. 5. Within weeks of his arrival in Jerusalem Nehemiah is to be found appointing city governors on his own account (7.2), which is evidently the responsibility of a provincial governor.

Some scholars see the force of these arguments, but the majority are reluctant to allow it; for they feel constrained by the narrative of ch. 2, which does not refer to any appointment of Nehemiah to the governorship. They are treating ch. 2 as a chronicle or even a tape-recording, from which the absence of a reference to the governorship would be meaningful. Chapter 2, however, is no such thing, but a narrative composed by Nehemiah to tell his readers only what he wants them to know, in the sequence he wants them to know it. There is a reticence here that may devolve from something in the psychology of Nehemiah, or else it may be a narratival ploy, or else it may be simply because the narrator is at this point in his narrative concentrating wholly upon the subject of wall-

1 The older view that Judaea was still subject to the Samarian authorities (so, e.g., Noth, *The History of Israel*, p. 322) seems now to have been given up by most. It is more common to see in Sheshbazzar and Zerubbabel the first of a line of governors of the province; for the possible archaeological evidence for a governor of Judaea between Zerubbabel and Nehemiah, see the well-nuanced comments of Williamson, pp. 243-44, and Blenkinsopp, pp. 263-64.

building—which evidently was always in Nehemiah's eyes his most enduring monument and his greatest claim to fame. We as historians do not need to know why it is that Nehemiah reserves any reference to his governorship to a point as late in the text as ch. 5; it is enough that he does so, and we must make up our minds about when his governorship began from the evidence we have and the balance of probabilities. To allow this judgment about historical probability to be conditioned by what is essentially a fictional narrative in 2.1-8 is to fall prey to Nehemiah's narrative art.

What happens in the scholarly literature is as follows: Noth avoids putting any date on the commencement of Nehemiah's governorship,[1] Myers casually drops the line, à propos of the conflict with Sanballat, that 'Nehemiah claimed to be the legitimate governor'[2] (was he or was he not?, we want to know), and Blenkinsopp comments that 'if the request for a leave of absence is historical, it does not seem that he was appointed governor before his departure from Susa, though he must have been shortly after his arrival in Jerusalem'.[3]

The last remark is the best, for it is hard to imagine that a man who left Susa without appointment to the governorship of Judaea should be found in that post within weeks of arrival in Jerusalem. Why Blenkinsopp, like others, cannot affirm that the balance of probability lies strongly with an appointment to that office before Nehemiah leaves Susa is because he does not want to deny that the narrative of ch. 2 is historical. Recognition that we are dealing in ch. 2 with a narrator who is composing a (to some extent) fictional narrative solves the problem; it does not mean that Nehemiah had no such interview with the king, but only that the course of the conversation was other than what the narration reports—which would not be in the least surprising. In short, what we have in 2.1-8 is not a piece of historical data that we can put side by side with the notation of 5.14 as if they were items of the same kind

---

1 'He appeared in Jerusalem ... with an official position which the king had conferred on him ... He became governor of the province of Judah' (*The History of Israel*, p. 321).
2 Myers, *The World of the Restoration*, p. 112.
3 Blenkinsopp, p. 262.

his toriographically speaking, but a fictionalized narrative whose historical worth is far different from that of the more formal reference in 5.14. It would be improper therefore to attempt to qualify the notation of 5.14 by reference to the narrative of 2.1-8.

4. *The Romantic Imagination*

There is another series of passages in the Nehemiah Memoir where the narrative can be credited only to what we must call the romantic imagination of the author. He knows so well how to tell a story and report a conversation that he has often managed to convince even the most acute of his critics that he is telling the unvarnished truth. For us to determine, however, how far we are willing to accept his account at face value, we have to examine the seeming implausibilities in the narrative. Only one such example of the implausible working of the romantic imagination will be considered under this heading: the account of the arming of the wall-builders.

The arming of the wall-builders (4.10-12 [EVV 16-18])
Nehemiah's depiction of the measure he took against any surprise attack by the Samarians and their allies has captured the popular imagination: the image of the sword and the trowel[1] is a powerful symbol that transfers itself easily to very different situations.[2] The question before us at the moment, however, is whether the account is historically plausible.

We should first distinguish the three groups of men mentioned, who are variously armed. There are first Nehemiah's own 'lads' (נערים) or personal servants, who were perhaps his police force or private army to which he was entitled as governor of the province. They had previously, it seems, been

---

1 It would be interesting to know when the concrete image of the 'trowel' originated; there is no trowel in Nehemiah's text, of course.
2 Cf., e.g., the line of T.S. Eliot, 'Remembering the words of Nehemiah the Prophet: "The trowel in hand, and the gun rather loose in the holster"' ('Choruses from "The Rock"', V, in *The Complete Plays and Poems of T.S. Eliot* [London: Faber and Faber, 1969], p. 158).

assigned to construction work, but now that Nehemiah has got wind of the threatened attack by Sanballat, he deploys half of them to guard duty,[1] and arms them quite comprehensively with the equipment of the Persian soldier, the short spear, wicker shield, the long bow, and the coat of iron mail. It would be strange if they did not also have the short sword, worn at the right hip; perhaps the word has dropped out through scribal accident, for the list begins oddly with 'and'.[2] The second group are the basket-carriers,[3] who, as they carried their loads on their heads or shoulders, would have hand one hand free for their 'weapon', lit. 'missile'—of what kind we cannot tell. The third group are the builders proper, who of course would need both hands free for their work, but could gird their short sword on out of the way.[4]

The historical question is simply whether it is possible to imagine workmen in the heat of the Jerusalem summer, who have obviously been urged to complete their task with all speed, encumbering themselves all day long with a weapon *when there is no enemy in sight and when lookouts have been posted*.[5] This does not appear to have been a question that has

1 Widengren incorrectly writes that Nehemiah 'divided the inhabitants into two divisions: one half working on the walls, the other half posted as guards' (p. 530); this division of course applied only to Nehemiah's נערים.

2 Cf. Clines, p. 164. Williamson thinks that the addition of 'swords' 'does not fit well with the view that this group was set apart specifically to carry the weapons which the wall builders could not carry, for we are told in v 12 (18) that swords were carried by all' (p. 222). On the contrary, the fact that swords are carried by others is no reason why they should not also have been carried by Nehemiah's 'lads', and the fact that they are more heavily armed than the builders themselves is no reason why they should not also carry the most immediately useful weapon of all, the sword.

3 For the translation of סבל, cf. Moshe Held, 'The Root *zbl/sbl* in Akkadian, Ugaritic and Biblical Hebrew', *JAOS* 88 (1968), pp. 90-96 (94-95).

4 We should note that this three-fold distinction has not always been evident; the Authorized Version, for example, implies that both the builders and the burden-bearers had one hand reserved for a weapon. It is now agreed, however, that the first two words of v. 11 (הבנים בחומה) should be transferred to v. 10 (cf. BHS).

5 Cf. Clines, p. 164: 'There may be some idealisation here; it is hard to imagine men working day after day under such a handicap

occurred to the commentators,[1] who have accepted Nehemiah's account at face value, adding only their own justifications of it.

Williamson, for example, writes that the basket-carriers 'had a hand free to carry a weapon with them—and this may well have been necessary as they moved in more exposed places outside the walls'.[2] Is it pedantic to ask just how when one is picking up—with both hands, presumably—a heavy load to carry on one's head or shoulder, one manages at the same time to pick up in one's hand a weapon.[3] Fensham thought it would be 'quite natural for men who work among the rubble to pick up a stone (missile) and carry it in one hand to defend themselves',[4] but when no enemy appeared on the horizon on any day of the wall-building it seems on the contrary to be most unnatural and unrealistic. Fensham further observes that 'Nehemiah wants to emphasize that the carriers were somehow hindered in their work by holding in one hand the basket and the other hand a weapon';[5] this may be an accurate statement of Nehemiah's intention as narrator, but it does not begin to address the question of whether such was truly what happened.

Once again we may surmise that the vigour of Nehemiah's narrative has unnerved commentators and prevented them from applying any yardstick of historical credibility to the account. But the question remains, if in this particular the narrative contains a manifest implausibility, at which other points does it—less obviously—misrepresent the actuality?

when no enemy was in sight'.

1 I have looked at Keil, Witton Davies, Ryle, Batten, Rudolph, Brockington, Myers, Ackroyd, Fensham, Kidner, Williamson, and Blenkinsopp.

2 Williamson, p. 228.

3 Keil thought that the burden-bearers 'could do their work with one hand, which would suffice for emptying rubbish into baskets, and for carrying material in handle baskets' (p. 205). It is hard to see how you can empty rubbish (presumably small stones) into a basket with one hand; and if indeed small baskets could have been used to carry the rubbish, it by no means follows that such *were* used, especially when urgency was the order of the day.

4 Fensham, p. 188, quoted by Williamson, p. 228.

5 Fensham, p. 188.

Having had our suspicions raised about this aspect of the text, can we continue, with undamaged confidence, to accept Nehemiah's word that 1. he had just one trumpeter to sound an alarm (v. 18), 2. that he kept the wall-builders in Jerusalem overnight for seven weeks, without allowing them to return home (v. 22), 3. that each worker had his own 'servant' (v. 22), 4. that Nehemiah did not take off his clothes except for washing during the seven weeks that the wall-building was in progress, and especially, 5. that the wall was actually finished in fifty-two days (6.15)? What do we actually *know*, as distinct from merely having reported to us by a canny narrator, about the building of the wall?

Conclusion

The present investigation has been an attempt to consider the Nehemiah Memoir from a literary perspective, focusing on one aspect of the work as a literary production, viz. the fact that it is a narrative told by a narrator who is also the author. And it has had in view the impact of this literary fact both upon readerly readers and upon readers who have never questioned the process of reading.

The constant tendency of this study has been to show that this literary fact and the readerly questions that it gives rise to have historical implications. It is indeed usual for practitioners of biblical literary criticism to insist that the literary must precede the historical, that we must understand the nature of our texts as literary works before we attempt to use them for historical reconstruction. This is my view too. But I must confess that in no literary study that I have previously done have the literary and the historical been so closely bound up, historical questions being raised—and sometimes answered—in the very process of asking the literary questions.

What has been evident also is that the literary facts of the composition have not been adequately considered in the history of the interpretation of the Book of Nehemiah, not even by the most eminent historians and commentators.[1]

---

1 I report in this connection some words of the English historian of the seventeenth century, Christopher Hill, in a radio interview

There has been a very strong tendency to take the Biblical writing at its face value and a disinclination to entertain a hermeneutic of suspicion such as is a prerequisite for serious historical investigation. It is shocking to see how the narrative of the Nehemiah Memoir has in fact been lazily adopted as a historiographical structure in the writing of modern scholars, and how rarely the question of the *probability* of the statements of the Nehemiah Memoir has been raised.[1] There has been in evidence a strong tendency to maximize the data, i.e. to claim a more thorough and certain knowledge of events of the period that even a modestly rigorous historical method would allow. No doubt it is possible for the modern historian to call into question quite a few claims of Nehemiah's which might, if the evidence existed, prove well-founded. But the task of the historian is not to accept the word of our written sources except where they can be proved erroneous, but to weigh everything in the same scale of probabilities, and pass judgments against implausibities even if a more coherent reconstruction of events cannot be proffered. It has been the intention of the present study to show that a strict regard to the literariness of the document and to the role of the reader in the processing of the document is inevitably profitable for the historian.

broadcast while I was editing this paper: 'You have to have a lot of literary criticism before you can understand a speech in Parliament, for example. Public records are not written to preserve truth, but to persuade people' (BBC Radio 3, November 7, 1989).

1 Particularly noticeable in this regard are the works of Myers, *The World of the Restoration*, pp. 108-22; Herrmann, pp. 310-14; Miller and Hayes, pp. 469-72; Widengren, pp. 528-32.

BIBLIOGRAPHY

Peter R. Ackroyd, *Israel under Babylon and Persia* (Oxford: Oxford University Press, 1970).
——*I & II Chronicles, Ezra, Nehemiah* (London: SCM Press, 1973).
Albrecht Alt, 'Die Rolle Samarias bei der Entstehung des Judentums', in *Festschrift Otto Procksch zum 60. Geburtstag* (Leipzig: A. Deichert & J.C. Hinrichs, 1934), pp. 5-28 (= *Kleine Schriften zur Geschichte des Volkes Israel* [München: Beck, 1953], vol. 2, pp. 316-37).
Robert Alter, 'Joseph and His Brothers', *Commentary* 70 (November, 1980), pp. 59-69.
——*The Art of Biblical Narrative* (London: George Allen and Unwin, 1981).
Thomas Aquinas, *Summa Theologiae. Latin text and English translation*, vol. 13, ed. Edmund Hill (London: Blackfriars in conjunction with Eyre and Spottiswoode, 1964).
Augustine, *De Genesi ad litteram libri duodecim* (= J.-P. Migne, *Patrologia Cursus Completus [Patrologia Latina]*, vol. 34 [Paris, 1845], cols. 245-486).
Mieke Bal, 'Sexuality, Sin and Sorrow: The Emergence of Female Character [A Reading of Genesis 2–3]', in *The Female Body in Western Culture*, ed. Susan Rubin Suleiman (Cambridge, MA: Harvard University Press, 1986), pp. 317-38.
Shimon Bar-Efrat, *Narrative Art in the Bible* (JSOTSup, 70; Bible and Literature Series, 17; Sheffield: Almond Press, 1989).
Loring W. Batten, *The Books of Ezra and Nehemiah* (ICC; Edinburgh: T. & T. Clark, 1913).
Adele Berlin, *Poetics and Interpretation of Biblical Narrative* (Bible and Literature Series, 9; Sheffield: Almond, 1983).
Phyllis Bird, 'Images of Women in the Old Testament', *The Bible and Human Liberation. Political and Social Hermeneutics*, ed. Norman K. Gottwald (Maryknoll, NY: Orbis, 1983), pp. 252-88.

————'"Male and Female He Created Them": Gen 1:27b in the Context of the Priestly Account of Creation', *HTR* 74 (1981), pp. 129-59.

————'Translating Sexist Language as a Theological and Cultural Problem', *USQR* 42 (1988), pp. 89-95.

Joseph Blenkinsopp, *Ezra–Nehemiah. A Commentary* (OTL; London: SCM Press, 1989).

Jorge Luis Borges, *Seven Nights* (tr. Eliot Weinberger; London: Faber and Faber, 1986).

Raymond A. Bowman, 'Ezra and Nehemiah', in *The Interpreter's Bible*, ed. George A. Buttrick, vol. 3 (Nashville: Abingdon, 1954), pp. 551-819.

John Bright, *A History of Israel* (3rd edn; London: SCM Press, 1981).

L.H. Brockington, *Ezra, Nehemiah and Esther* (NCB; London: Nelson, 1969).

Walter Brueggemann, 'The Kerygma of the Priestly Writers', *ZAW* 84 (1972), pp. 397-414.

———*Genesis: A Bible Commentary for Teaching and Preaching* (Atlanta: John Knox Press, 1982).

John Calvin, *A Commentary on Genesis* (tr. John King; London: Banner of Truth Trust, 1965).

David J.A. Clines, *The Theme of the Pentateuch* (JSOTSup, 10; Sheffield: JSOT Press, 1978).

———*Ezra, Nehemiah, Esther* (NCB; London: Marshall, Morgan & Scott, 1984).

————'Introduction to the Biblical Story: Genesis–Esther', in *Harper's Bible Commentary*, ed. James L. Mays (San Francisco: Harper and Row, 1988), pp. 74-84.

————'Job', in *The Books of the Bible*, ed. B.W. Anderson (New York: Charles Scribner's Sons, 1989), pp. 181-201.

————*Job 1–20* (WBC, 17; Waco, Texas: Word Books, 1989).

————'Deconstructing the Book of Job', in *The Bible and Rhetoric. Studies in Biblical Persuasion and Credibility*, ed. Martin Warner (Warwick Studies in Philosophy and Literature; London: Routledge, 1990), pp. 65-80.

————'Reading Esther from Left to Right: Contemporary Strategies for Reading a Biblical Text', in *The Bible in Three Dimensions. Essays in Celebration of the Fortieth Anniversary of the Department of*

Biblical Studies, University of Sheffield, ed. David J.A. Clines, Stephen E. Fowl and Stanley E. Porter (JSOTSup, 87; Sheffield: JSOT Press, 1990), pp. 31-52.

——'The Story of Michal in its Sequential Unfolding', in David J.A. Clines and Tamara C. Eskenazi, *Michal, Wife of David: A Multi-voiced Telling of her Story* (Sheffield: JSOT Press, forthcoming).

George W. Coats, *Genesis: With an Introduction to Narrative Literature* (FOTL, 1; Grand Rapids: Eerdmans, 1983).

Frank Moore Cross, *Canaanite Myth and Hebrew Epic. Essays in the History of the Religion of Israel* (Cambridge, MA: Harvard University Press, 1973).

Jonathan Culler, *On Deconstruction. Theory and Criticism after Structuralism* (London: Routledge & Kegan Paul, 1983).

T. Witton Davies, *Ezra, Nehemiah and Esther* (CentB; Edinburgh: T.C. & E.C. Jack, 1909).

Samuel R. Driver, *The Book of Genesis* (WC; London: Methuen, 12th edn, 1926).

Terry Eagleton, *Literary Theory. An Introduction* (Oxford: Basil Blackwell, 1983).

Umberto Eco, *The Role of the Reader. Explorations in the Semiotics of Texts* (London: Hutchison & Co., 1981).

Alfred Einstein, *Mozart. His Character, His Work* (tr. Arthur Mendel and Nathan Broder; London: Cassell, 1946).

Otto Eissfeldt, *The Old Testament. An Introduction* (tr. Peter R. Ackroyd; Oxford: Basil Blackwell, 1966).

Tamara C. Eskenazi, *In an Age of Prose. A Literary Approach to Ezra–Nehemiah* (SBLMS, 36; Atlanta: Scholars Press, 1988).

F. Charles Fensham, *The Books of Ezra and Nehemiah* (NICOT; Grand Rapids: Eerdmans, 1982).

Stanley E. Fish, 'Interpreting the *Variorum*', *Critical Inquiry* 2 (1976), pp. 465-85; reprinted in his *Is There a Text in this Class? The Authority of Interpretive Communities* (Cambridge, MA: Harvard University Press, 1980), pp. 147-73, and in *Reader-Response Criticism. From Formalism to Post-Structuralism*, ed. Jane Tompkins (Baltimore: Johns Hopkins University Press, 1980), pp. 164-84.

——'Literature in the Reader: Affective Stylistics', *New Literary*

History 2 (Autumn, 1970), pp. 123-62 (= his *Self-Consuming Artifacts* [Berkeley: University of California Press, 1972], pp. 383-427).

D.W. Fokkema and Elrud Kunne-Ibsch, *Theories of Literature in the Twentieth Century. Structuralism, Marxism, Aesthetics of Reception, Semiotics* (London: C. Hurst, 1978).

David Noel Freedman, 'Deuteronomic History, The', in *The Interpreter's Dictionary of the Bible. Supplementary Volume*, ed. K. Crim (Nashville: Abingdon, 1976), pp. 226-28.

——'The Earliest Bible', in Michael P. O'Connor and D.N. Freedman (eds.), *Backgrounds for the Bible* (Winona Lake, IN: Eisenbrauns, 1987), pp. 29-37.

Elizabeth Freund, *The Return of the Reader. Reader-response Criticism* (London: Methuen, 1987).

Edward L. Greenstein, *Essays on Biblical Method and Translation* (Brown Judaic Studies, 92; Atlanta: Scholars Press, 1989).

David M. Gunn, 'Reading Right. Reliable and Omniscient Narrator, Omniscient God, and Foolproof Composition in the Hebrew Bible', *The Bible in Three Dimensions. Essays in Celebration of Forty Years of Biblical Studies in the University of Sheffield*, ed. David J.A. Clines, Stephen E. Fowl and Stanley E. Porter (JSOTSup, 87; Sheffield: JSOT Press, 1990), pp. 53-64.

John C.L. Gibson, *Genesis* (DSB; Edinburgh: Saint Andrew Press, 1982), 2 vols.

Gregory the Great, *Moralia in Job*, ed. M. Adriaen (Corpus Christianorum. Series Latina, 143, 143A, 143B; Turnhout: Brepols, 1979-85), 3 vols. In English: *Morals on the Book of Job* (tr. James Bliss; Oxford: H. Parker, 1844-50).

Moshe Held, 'The Root *zbl/sbl* in Akkadian, Ugaritic and Biblical Hebrew', *JAOS* 88 (1968), pp. 90-96

Siegfried Herrmann, *A History of Israel in Old Testament Times* (London: SCM Press, 1975).

Robert C. Holub, *Reception Theory. A Critical Introduction* (London: Methuen, 1984).

Wolfgang Iser, *The Act of Reading. A Theory of Aesthetic Response* (Eng. tr.; Baltimore: Johns Hopkins Univerity Press, 1978).

Hans Robert Jauss, *Toward an Aesthetic of Reception* (tr. Timothy Bahti;

Brighton: The Harvester Press, 1982).

Ann Jefferson and David Robey, *Modern Literary Theory. A Comparative Introduction*(London: Batsford Academic and Educational Ltd, 1982).

Carl F. Keil, *The Books of Ezra, Nehemiah, and Esther* (tr. Sophie Taylor; Clark's Foreign Theological Library. Fourth Series, 38; Edinburgh: T. & T. Clark, 1873).

Ulrich Kellermann, *Nehemia. Quellen, Überlieferung und Geschichte* (BZAW, 102; Berlin: A. Töpelmann, 1967).

Derek Kidner, *Genesis. An Introduction and Commentary* (TOTC; London: Tyndale Press, 1967).

——*Ezra and Nehemiah* (TOTC; Leicester: Inter-Varsity Press, 1979).

Susan S. Lanser, '(Feminist) Criticism in the Garden: Inferring Genesis 2–3', in *Speech Act Theory and Biblical Criticism*, ed. Hugh C. White (Decatur, GA: Scholars Press, 1988) (= *Semeia* 41 [1988], pp. 67-84).

David Lodge (ed.), *Modern Criticism and Theory. A Reader* (London: Longman, 1988).

Eric I. Lowenthal, letter in *Commentary* 71 (February, 1981), pp. 17-18.

J.Gordon McConville, *Ezra, Nehemiah and Esther* (DSB; Edinburgh: St Andrew Press, 1985).

Edgar V. McKnight, *The Bible and the Reader. An Introduction to Literary Criticism* (Philadelphia: Fortress, 1985).

Edgar V. McKnight, *Post-Modern Use of the Bible. The Emergence of Reader-Oriented Criticism* (Nashville: Abingdon, 1988).

J. Maxwell Miller and John H. Hayes, *A History of Ancient Israel and Judah* (London: SCM Press, 1986).

John W. Miller, 'Depatriarchalizing God in Biblical Interpretation: A Critique', *CBQ* 48 (1986), pp. 609-16.

Peter D. Miscall, 'The Jacob and Joseph Stories as Analogies', *JSOT* 6 (1978), pp. 28-40.

——*The Workings of Old Testament Narrative* (SBL Semeia Series; Philadelphia: Fortress Press, 1983).

Sigmund Mowinckel, *Studien zu dem Buche Ezra–Nehemia* (Oslo: Universitetsforlaget, 1964), vol. 2.

Jacob M. Myers, *Ezra, Nehemiah* (AB, 14; Garden City, NY: Doubleday, 1965).

————*The World of the Restoration* (Englewood Cliffs, NJ: Prentice-Hall, 1968).

Martin Noth, *The History of Israel* (London: A. & C. Black, 2nd edn, 1960).

————*The Deuteronomistic History* (tr. Jane Doull *et al.*; JSOTSup, 15; Sheffield: JSOT Press, 1981 [original edition: *Überlieferungsgeschichtliche Studien* (Schriften der Königsberger Gelehrten Gesellschaft. Geisteswissenschaftliche Klasse, 18; Halle: Max Niemeyer Verlag, 1943), pp. 1-110).

W.O.E. Oesterley, *A History of Israel*, vol. 2 (Oxford: Clarendon Press, 1932).

David L. Petersen, 'A Thrice-Told Tale: Genre, Theme and Motif in Genesis 12, 20 and 26', *Biblical Research* 18 (1973), pp. 30-43.

Robert Polzin, '"The Ancestress in Danger" in Danger', *Semeia* 3 (1975), pp. 81-98.

————*Moses and the Deuteronomist. A Literary Study of the Deuteronomic History, Part One: Deuteronomy, Joshua, Judges* (New York: Seabury, 1980).

————*Samuel and the Deuteronomist. A Literary Study of the Deuteronomistic History, Part Two: 1 Samuel* (San Francisco: Harper & Row, 1989).

Marvin H. Pope, *Job* (AB, 15; Garden City, NY: Doubleday, 3rd edn, 1973).

Gerhard von Rad, *Genesis. A Commentary* (OTL; revised edn; Philadelphia: Westminster, 1972).

George W. Ramsey, 'Is Name-Giving an Act of Domination in Genesis 2:23 and Elsewhere?', *CBQ* 50 (1988), pp. 24-35.

William Ray, *Literary Meaning. From Phenomenology to Deconstruction* (Oxford: Basil Blackwell, 1984).

Wolfgang Richter, 'Traum und Traumdeutung im AT: Ihre Form und Verwendung', *Biblische Zeitschrift* 7 (1963), pp. 202-20.

Alexander Roberts and James Donaldson (eds.), *The Clementine Homilies. The Apostolical Constitutions* (Ante-Nicene Christian Library, 17; Edinburgh: T. and T. Clark, 1870).

Wilhelm Rudolph, *Esra und Nehemia* (HAT, 20; Tübingen: J.C.B. Mohr, 1949).

Letty M. Russell, 'Authority and the Challenge of Feminist Interpretation', in *Feminist Interpretation of the Bible*, ed. Letty M. Russell (Oxford: Blackwell, 1985), pp. 137-49.

Rick Rylance (ed.), *Debating Texts. A Reader in Twentieth-Century Literary Theory and Method* (Milton Keynes: Open University Press, 1987).

Herbert E. Ryle, *The Books of Ezra and Nehemiah* (CamB; Cambridge: Cambridge University Press, 1893).

Donald A. Seybold, 'Paradox and Symmetry in the Joseph Narrative', in *Literary Interpretations of Biblical Narratives*, ed. Kenneth R.R. Gros Louis *et al.* (Nashville: Abingdon Press, 1974), vol. 1, pp. 59-73.

John Skinner, *A Critical and Exegetical Commentary on Genesis* (ICC; Edinburgh: T. and T. Clark, 2nd edn, 1930).

Ephraim A. Speiser, *Genesis* (AB, 1; Garden City, NY: Doubleday, 1983).

Elizabeth Cady Stanton, *The Woman's Bible: The Original Feminist Attack on the Bible* (Edinburgh: Polygon Books, 1985; abridgment of the original edition, New York: European Publishing Co., 1895, 1898).

Krister Stendahl, 'Biblical Theology' in *The Interpreter's Dictionary of the Bible,* ed. George A. Buttrick (Nashville: Abingdon, 1962), vol. 1, pp. 418-32.

Meir Sternberg, *The Poetics of Biblical Narrative: Ideological Literature and the Drama of Reading* (Bloomington: Indiana University Press, 1985).

J. Strahan, *The Book of Job Interpreted* (Edinburgh: T. and T. Clark, 1913).

Susan R. Suleiman and Inge Crosman, *The Reader in the Text. Essays on Audience and Interpretation* (Princeton: Princeton University Press, 1980).

Jane Tompkins, *Reader-Response Criticism. From Formalism to Post-Structuralism* (Baltimore: Johns Hopkins University Press, 1980).

Phyllis Trible, 'Depatriarchalizing in Biblical Interpretation', *JAAR* 41 (1973), pp. 30-48.

———*God and the Rhetoric of Sexuality* (Philadelphia: Fortress Press, 1978).

———'Genesis 2–3 Revisited', in *Womanspirit Rising: A Feminist Reader on Religion*, ed. Carol Christ and Judith Plaskow (New York: Harper and Row, 1975).

Laurence A. Turner, 'Lot as Jekyll and Hyde', in *The Bible in Three Dimensions. Essays in Celebration of Forty Years of Biblical*

Studies in the University of Sheffield, ed. David J.A. Clines, Stephen E. Fowl and Stanley E. Porter (JSOTSup, 87; Sheffield: JSOT Press, 1990), pp. 85-98.

——*Announcements of Plot in Genesis* (JSOTSup, 96; Sheffield: JSOT Press, 1990).

Mark Twain, *Extracts from Adam's Diary* (New York: Harper & Bros., 1906).

John van Seters, *Abraham in History and Tradition* (London: Yale University Press, 1975).

Theodorus C. Vriezen, 'Bemerkungen zu Genesis 12.1-7', in Martinus A. Beek *et al.* (eds.), *Symbolae biblicae et Mesopotamicae Francisco Mario Theodoro de Liagre Böhl dedicatae* (Leiden: E.J. Brill, 1973).

R.A. Watson, *The Book of Job* (ExpB; London: Hodder and Stoughton, 1892).

Claus Westermann, *Genesis 1–11. A Commentary* (tr. John J. Scullion; Minneapolis: Augsburg, 1984).

——*Genesis 12–36. A Commentary* (tr. John J. Scullion; Minneapolis: Augsburg, 1985).

Geo Widengren, 'The Persian Period', in *Israelite and Judean History*, ed. John H. Hayes and J. Maxwell Miller (OTL; London: SCM Press, 1977), pp. 489-538.

Hugh G.M. Williamson, *Ezra, Nehemiah* (WBC, 16; Waco, Texas: Word Books, 1985).

INDEX OF AUTHORS

INDEX OF BIBLICAL REFERENCES

JOURNAL FOR THE STUDY OF THE OLD TESTAMENT
Supplement Series